Motherhood
....Through a Year of Pregnancy

Parvesh Handa
Exceptional Assistance & Medical Tips by

Dr. D.S. Jaspal
National Vice Chairman, Indian Medical Association

Dr. Reeta Jaspal
Senior Gynaecologist & President IMA-Haryana

Published by:

F-2/16, Ansari Road, Daryaganj, New Delhi-110002
☎ 011-23240026, 011-23240027 • *Fax:* 011-23240028
Email: info@vspublishers.com • *Website:* www.vspublishers.com

Regional Office : Hyderabad
5-1-707/1, Brij Bhawan (Beside Central Bank of India Lane)
Bank Street, Koti, Hyderabad - 500 095
☎ 040-24737290
E-mail: vspublishershyd@gmail.com

Branch Office : Mumbai
Flat No. Ground Floor, Sonmegh Building
No. 51, Karel Wadi, Thakurdwar, Mumbai - 400 002
☎ 022-22098268
E-mail: vspublishersmum@gmail.com

Follow us on: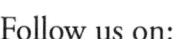

For any assistance sms **VSPUB** to **56161**
All books available at **www.vspublishers.com**

© Copyright: Author
ISBN 978-93-813849-9-2
Edition 2014

The Copyright of this book, as well as all matter contained herein (including illustrations) rests with the Publisher. No person shall copy the name of the book, its title design, matter and illustrations in any form and in any language, totally or partially or in any form. Anybody doing so shall face legal action and will be responsible for damages.

Printed at : Param Offseters Okhla New Delhi-110020

Publisher's Note

V&S Publishers has successfully published a number of books on Women and Child Health and is glad to publish yet another book, especially for Pregnant Women named **Motherhood**. The book is a complete guide on *Pregnancy and Motherhood* and has been authored by an experienced and veteran writer, Parvesh Handa, who is also a *renowned cosmetologist*, researching and preparing women's beauty products, especially made up of herbs and roots.

She has more than *44 books to her credit on women-related subjects*, such as beauty culture, fashion, modelling, women's health, slimming, naturopathy, yoga, etc.

She is also the author of one of our best-sellers, *Home Beauty Clinic,* and hence, has been chosen to be the one to write this valuable book on Motherhood giving a complete detailed knowledge on the Important Facts Prior to Conception and After the Conception of a Baby, the Various Trimesters of Pregnancy, Different Types of Labour and Deliveries, Diet and Exercises a Woman should undertake Before and After Childbirth, Diseases that Commonly Affect a Pregnant Woman and their Preventions, etc.

Hence readers, this book answers all your queries regarding *Pregnancy* and *Childbirth* covering *A-Z on the subject,* and is a *Must Read* for all, particularly, the women section of the society and the ones going to be a Mother for the first time!

Disclaimer

This book is not intended to take the place of medical advice from a trained medical professional. Readers are advised to consult a qualified doctor or a gynaecologist regarding treatment of their medical problems. Neither the author, nor the publisher takes any responsibility for any possible consequences from any treatment, action or application of medicine, herb or preparation to any person reading or following the information in this book.

Preface

'Planning for a baby is a pleasure and joy and on the other hand, a duty and responsibility.' Hence, correct knowledge provides an expectant woman not only a painless delivery, but also a healthy and jubilant baby. This book is one such effort to provide a handy help to pregnant women, especially those going to be mother for the first time.

During pregnancy, the expectant mothers should see her doctor at least once a month to get herself examined to make sure that the foetus is developing satisfactorily. Besides, she needs to do a lot herself and this book tells all that. Various problems faced by a pregnant woman prior to conception, during pregnancy, labour and after delivering the child have been described in this book in detail.

Ms. Parvesh Handa receiving the Micro Small and Medium Enterprises (MSME) National Award for the year, 2012 in the MSME Sector on March 1, 2014 at Vigyan Bhawan, New Delhi.

Thanks to the amazing advances of medical science, the discomforts connected with pregnancy have become much easier to cope with, and with a little care, you can make your pregnancy and life enjoyable. So it is no longer time to worry about or brood over but to plan and dream.

I am thankful to medical experts and gynecologists for the cooperation and assistance in writing this book useful for the pregnant women and those ailing from genital disorders. The readers should keep in mind that medical treatments referred in this book are for reference only, and it is neither a medical guide nor a manual of self-treatment. No medical treatment should be taken without consultation with a qualified doctor.

Dear Readers, It gives me great pleasure to inform all of you that after years of incessant work, I have been awarded the *MSME (Micro, Small & Medium Enterprises) National Award* for the *year, 2012* for my outstanding performance in the *MSME Sector, as acknowledged by the Government of India*. The prestigious Award was presented to me by the *Hon'ble Prime Minister of India, Dr. Mammohan Singh and the Hon'ble Minister, MSME in the National Awards Function that was held at 10.00 A.M. on Saturday, the 1st of March, 2014 at the Plenary Hall, Vigyan Bhawan, New Delhi.*

–*Parvesh Handa*

Contents

Chapter : 1
Important Facts Prior to Conception 9

Chapter : 2
First Trimester of Pregnancy 27

Chapter : 3
Second Trimester of Pregnancy 42

Chapter : 4
Third Trimester of Pregnancy 56

Chapter : 5
Three Stages of Labour 68

Chapter : 6
Beautiful Body During & After Pregnancy 83

Chapter : 7
Breast & Breastfeeding 96

Chapter : 8
AIDS 105

Chapter : 9
Vaginal Diseases 108

Chapter : 10
Important Tips for the New Born 120

Chapter 1

Important Facts Prior to Conception

I am getting married shortly, but I am unaware about the functioning of various genital parts of the body. I feel shy to know from my mother. Can you brief me about it?

Every woman, before getting married should know about the functioning of different genital parts in the body. I have come across several women getting married or expectant mothers having the least knowledge of their own body organs. Many teenagers, even the newly married women feel hesitant to ask questions about the male or female genital organs, though their knowledge is essential for a happy married life and make pregnancy painless, enjoyable and healthy. Following is a brief description of the important body organs playing a significant role during pregnancy.

The *Vulva* is an ill-defined area, which in gynaecological practice comprises the whole of the external genitalia. A woman's perineum includes the pelvic floor muscles, external genitalia, urethra, anus and portion between the vagina and the anus. The external genitalia include the vaginal opening, clitoris, labia majora, labia minora and mono pubis – the fatty tissue over the pubic bone.

The *mons pubis* is the visible part of the genital organ when in the upright posture with cushion of fat in the front and is covered with curly hair after puberty. It has two outer lips of the vulva called the

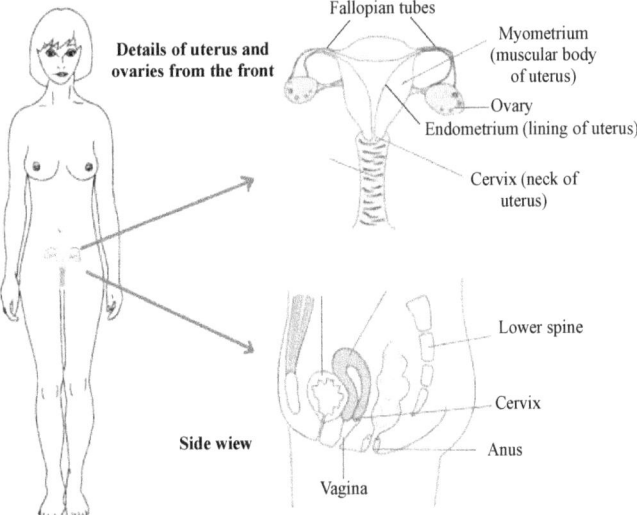

Various Genital Parts of a Female Body

labia majora. After the age of 16, hair appears at the outer surface of the labia majora and sometimes on the *perineum skin*. The inner surface of the pinkish coloured labia majora is the soft, moist, hairless and pinkish coloured body having the *sebaceous glands, sweat glands* and *hair follicles* liable to common skin disorders, such as *lesions, boils* and *cysts*.

The *labia minora* lies on the inner aspect of the *labia majora*: a thin fold of skin without the sebaceous glands or hair follicles but have veins and elastic tissue, which erect during sexual activity. The *Bartholin's Gland* is a compound measuring about 10 mm in diameter and about 25 mm long, secreting lubricating mucus during *coitus*.

The *clitoris* consists of glands covered by the *prepuce* and a body which is subcutaneous that corresponds to the male penis attached to the under surface of the *pubis*. The *clitoris* is extremely sensitive and during coitus, it becomes erect playing a considerable part in inducing the *orgasm of the female*.

The **Uterus** also called the **womb** is a compartment in the female body in which a baby forms and grows till birth. A pear-shaped hollow thick walled muscular organ situated in the pelvis behind the bladder and in front of the rectum, deep in the lower abdomen is divided into two parts: The upper part called the *body* and the lower part called the *cervix*, which protrudes into the *vagina*.

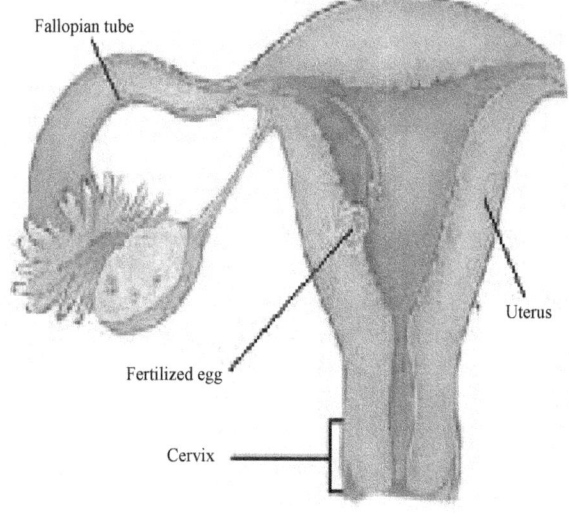

Uterus

The *uterus* is about 3"x2"x1" in size in non-pregnant state and gradually stretches to accommodate a fully formed baby. The size and shape of a normal uterus varies, such as an *infantile uterus* ranges from 2 to 3.3 cm. in length with 0.5 to 1 cm in diameter. The weight of a virgin's uterus is usually 42 gm and the *pear-shaped uterus* gradually increases in size with the advancement of pregnancy.

Fallopian Tubes extend from the upper side of the uterus towards the ovaries located on each side of the uterus. *Ovaries produce sex glands:* Estrogen, Progesterone and the Female Sex Hormones. Estrogen stimulates the development of secondary sexual characteristics, such as enlarged breasts, body hair in females, etc. The ovaries also ripen and expel the ova known as the *eggs*.

How conception and pregnancy take place?

After sexual intercourse, the sperm travels from the vagina through the cervix into the cavity of the uterus along the fallopian tubes. *Conception takes place when a single sperm penetrates or fertilizes an ovum, forming a single cell.* Although, large numbers of sperms ejaculate and reach the ovum, only one penetrates it and once the ovum is fertilized, a chemical reaction occurs preventing

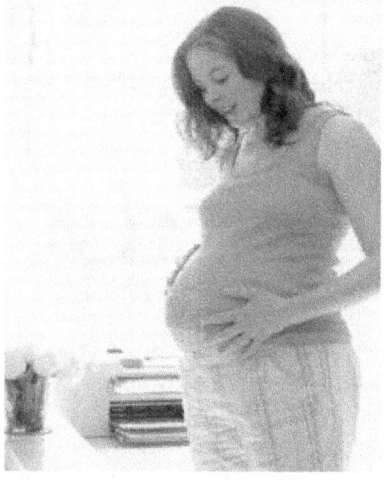

A Pregnant Woman

other sperms from penetrating. After fertilization, the ovum travels along the fallopian tube and embeds within the uterus giving the baby unique inherited characteristics, such as skin, hair and eye colour, height, body shape, type of blood, sex, etc. About 4" in length, the vagina runs from the cervix between the bladder and the rectum unites with the uterus and the vulva, an important organ in the female body. The upper broad end of the uterus opens on either side into two long tubes, called the *fallopian tubes* varying from 7 to 12 cm. in length, each ending in a funnel-shaped opening guarded by five finger-like projections.

What is the role of Penis in a male body?
The Penis is the *male genital organ* that serves a dual function of *erection and excretion of urine and semen.* It is composed of *three cylindrical structures of cavernous.* The blood supply to the penis is primarily made through arteries at the base of the penis, which supply blood to the skin and glands of the penis. Until recently, it was felt that psychological factors cause *male impotency.* However, studies have revealed that a majority of the cases of impotency have organic causes. Studies reveal, *Vasculogenic impotence* is due to poor arterial inflow into the penis causing *erection failure. Venogenic impotence* is caused due to leakage of blood in the penis. According to experts, the prominent causes of impotence are *Vasculogenic* (37.5% cases), *Diabetes mellitus* (20% cases), *Psychogenic* (11.7%), *Neurogenic* (6.7%), *Malignancy* (5.8% cases), *Testoterone and Trauma* (3.3% cases) and other cases (11.7%).

What is the functioning of ovary disorders in female body and how to detect such disorders?
The Ovary is 1.5 inches long, 0.75 inches broad resembling like a *pigeon egg*. It has an appearance of almond-shaped flattened bodies connected with the base of the uterus by ligament tightly attached to the *fallopian tubes. Polycystic ovary disease* cause disorders like *Amenorrhea (menstruation disorders), Hirsutism* (excess superfluous hair on the body), *Obesity and Infertility,* Formation of *Cysts, Pelvic Inflammatory Disease or Tumour* and *Ovary Cancer.* Remember, *Sexually Transmitted Diseases (STD)* cause *pain, fever* and *vaginal discharge. Ultrasound* and *Laproscopy* are popular methods to detect *ovarian disorders.*

I've problem of having varicose veins in upper legs and thighs. How to cure?
Enlarged superficial veins in and around the legs and thighs due to increased pressure on veins lose elasticity and become elongated. As blood returns to the heart through thin-walled channels called *veins*, these vessels are easily distended and swell as the blood builds up behind it. Blood flows towards the heart from the head as well as from the lower extremities, it flows upwards. To make it possible, nature has provided *valves* in the *veins* to make blood flow towards the heart. *Constipation, smoking* and *hot baths* are some of the factors to cause *varicose veins.*

The valves of the *varicose veins* in the legs, especially around the ankles and valves,

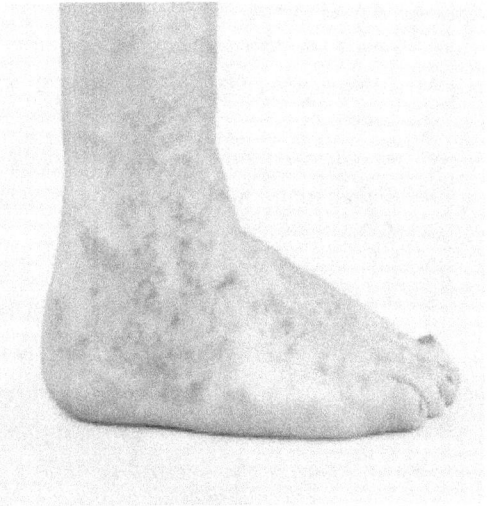

Varicose Veins

thighs are incompetent to prevent the *backflow of blood* resulting in stagnation followed by as well as the *swelling, pain, inflammation or phlebitis*. Standing for a long time, while suffering from varicose veins lead to reduced blood supply to the muscles. This ailment is more frequent in pregnancy and obesity due to increased pressure in the pelvis or abdominal region, which slows the flow of blood to the heart from the lower extremities. The following measures are suggested to treat *varicose veins:*

- Check weight. Extra amount of weight increases pressure on venous circulation.
- Blood sugar should remain within the prescribed limits.
- Avoid prolonged standing.
- Wear comfortable padded low-heel shoes.
- Wear varicose vein stockings available at a chemist or surgical store.
- A hot and cold footbath before bedtime improves blood circulation and prevents varicose veins.
- Walking or jogging in water is very helpful to relieve varicose veins.
- Vitamin C strengthens the vein walls (2,000 to 3000 mg daily).
- Rosemary tea with honey and elderflower tea are old-fashioned remedies to aid the circulation.
- Raise the legs several times a day and sleep with the foot of the bed raised six to eight inches higher than the head side.
- Massage the legs gently but *do not scratch the varicose veins* because the varicose ulcers may result in from a sore place. *Excellent massage oils for varicose veins* are *olive oil, sweet almond oil, essential oils of cypress, calendula, rosemary* and *lavender.*
- Regular practice of *yoga* relieves *varicose veins* and *cramps.*

I suffer from the problem of excessive thick yellow vaginal discharge. Suggest remedies.

It is common in females of every age when a *yellowish discharge from vagina* accompanied by itching can be due to *fungal or bacterial infection*. Consult your doctor immediately. There is great need of cleanliness of the genital area prior to or during pregnancy. Some of the common warning signs during pregnancy include:

- Vaginal bleeding posing threats of miscarriage, placenta previa or premature labour.
- Leakage of fluid from vagina may cause rupture of membranes.
- Pain/burning while urinating, generally due to urinary tract infection. Sexually transmitted disease.
- Irritating vaginal discharge due to urinary tract infection.
- Soreness or itching with discharge posing threat of sexually transmitted disease.

I was married a year ago and have conceived, but got it aborted since we were not interested to become parents so early. After the first abortion, I suffered from yellow discharge and the doctor suggested Candid V6 and V3 but the discharge persists even after the second abortion. Besides, I have pain on the left side near the rectum, while passing urine. Please suggest a remedy.

The prominent cause of yellow discharge can be due to *infection: fungal or bacterial. Candid V6/V3 is used for treating fungal infection,* or bacterial infection. Other medicines are also useful. Get a high *vaginal swab* for culture sensitivity done. A *PAP smear* would be helpful. Consult a doctor.

My 10 years old younger sister recently had first menses at the age less than 10. Please advise if a girl at this age can develop pregnancy?

If menses have begun at this age, it means *neuro-hormonal mechanism* have started functioning and the ovaries are producing eggs. *So, a pregnancy is possible. Initially, her periods would be irregular and heavy due to her hormonal imbalance.* However the periods become regular within few months.

I am getting married soon, but have very loose vaginal muscle. What should I do?

This sometimes, ruins many happy marriages. Remember, *one cannot prove that women with loose vaginal muscles are not virgin, nor these muscles would be an hindrance in satisfying the male partner. Practice of yoga and exercises help relief.* 'Vajroli Mudra' is a yogic posture, which helps to tighten and strengthen the loose vaginal muscles, relieve the disorders of pelvic region and strengthen all the sex organs among both the sexes. This exercise strengthens the anterior and the posterior parts of the pubic muscles. A pregnant woman should do about 5 to 6 rounds of this posture daily, strictly in consultation with the doctor.

To practise *Vajroli Mudra*, sit in *Padma Asana* (Lotus Pose) or any comfortable meditative *asana*. Place your hands on the knees, close your eyes, feel relaxed and breathe through the nose. After a deep inhalation, hold your breath and try to draw the sexual organs upward by pulling and tensing the lower abdomen contracting the pelvic muscles, as if one has an urge to pass urine but wishes to hold one for some time. *Now exhale, relax and repeat the posture.* This posture also helps those suffering from *premature ejaculation* and *delay climaxing (orgasm)* when involved in intercourse.

I am 30, married but without any issue. I have the habit of masturbating since the age of 16. I also have white non-smelling discharge before periods, but there is no itching. Is it due to masturbation?

A little vaginal discharge before periods is common due to changes that occur in the *cervical mucosa* taking place at this time. It is not due to *masturbation*, rest assured. Masrturbation is a harmless habit. *Staphysagria pills* taken twice a day are useful to control masturbation. However, consult a doctor before taking pills.

I have lost the sex drive after I had hysterectomy due to a recurring yeast infection. My ovaries were not removed and are working fine. I am disturbed, because my husband is still sexually very active. Prior to surgery, our sex life was normal.

Light Exercises

What to do?
Probably, the surgery did something to prevent the hormones secreted by the ovaries from entering your system. Better consult a counsellor to clarify whether the surgery caused a mental block of some kind.

I got married two days earlier and never had sexual intercourse before. In spite of being a virgin, I didn't bleed during my first intercourse last night and was anticipating bleeding due to the rupture of the hymen?

It is a myth that one should bleed during the first intercourse. The *hymen is a thin membrane* that covers the vagina. It may or may not be present at the birth. Moreover, by certain activities like sports or athletics, it may also get broken. Even masturbation breaks the hymen in some cases.

We are married for a year. My husband gets visibly upset whenever, I cannot reach orgasm, even though I don't mind. But how do I explain this to him?

Lots of women are pressurised by their partners, and even themselves, to reach *orgasm*. Men carry certain guilt for climaxing without the partner climaxing too. Men need to know that the goal of sex is to be gentle and loving to each other. They usually tend to forget that *physical closeness and sharing of feelings during a good foreplay with a loved one is a pleasure.*

I'm not having periods but feel pain during periods every month?

It may be due to a *closed hymen*. Sexually well-developed teenage females sometimes do not have menses despite good health, although they feel periodic pains in the vaginal area for few days every month besides having severe pain in the lower belly during the period days. In few cases, an ultrasound report shows a completely closed hymen. *Surgical operation helps to start normal periods. So consult a doctor.*

Does marriage in blood relations leave a bad effect?

Marriage between blood relations is genetically unhealthy, as both father and mother may carry the same type of unhealthy genes, which could intensify the unhealthy manifestation in the offsprings. Here is an example of a known couple, both were closely related having blood relation. Their first baby was *mentally retarded*. They had an *abnormal second baby*. The *third, a premature*, died soon after the birth. The fourth also born premature was too, far from normal.

What should be the duration of having sex?

It depends upon the couples to involve into a pattern to suit their moods and needs. The frequency of the relationship varies from couple to couple. Some need sex everyday, others once or twice a month even in their early stage of marriage. With increasing age, there is a rapir decline in sex in most of the couples. *During pregnancy, frequent sex is not advisable* and a couple must seek advice of a gynaecologist. In case of *problematic pregnancy*, better avoid sex as far as possible. In case of blood spots, do not indulge in sex, this may lead to abortion.

I am just married. What is honeymoon urethritis?

Overenthusiastic love making, excessive handling of clitoris during foreplay and *frequent intercourse*, lead to *severe inflammation of the urethral opening resulting in honeymoon urethritis*. If the vagina has become infected or the infection is severe, pus cells pass into the bladder. Consult a doctor immediately for treatment.

Is excessive breast sucking by the husband harmful?

Sucking of breast by the husband is not harmful. If husband wishes to suck the breasts, he should not be discouraged. This is natural and healthy exercise for the nipples and the breasts.

I want to avoid having baby for a year or two, suggest natural contraceptive methods.

Easy *contraceptive methods for family planning* are of *three types* as described below:

Coitus interrupts: This is an *unreliable and unhealthy method of contraception* usually practised by *traditional couples* in which the sex act is interrupted at the time of male ejaculation and the male organ is quickly withdrawn out of the vagina before the semen is discharged out. However, long-term practice of *coitus interrupts* can cause pelvic congestion with the formation of *ovarian cysts* in females.

Rhythm method: This method follows the *natural ovulation* pattern in women, which happens once a month on the *14th day of the cycle* (immediately before and after this day are the most fertile days for ovulation). However, the days following the menses and preceding the next period are the least fertile. The ovum is capable of getting fertilised for two or three days after its liberation as the discharged sperms remain vital for three or four days in the upper regions of the female genital tract. *If the intercourse is avoided during ovulation and three to four days before and after, the chances of conception are minimal*. The husband's cooperation is very necessary to avoid having sex for over a week in the mid - cycle or use a condom during this period.

Lactating the baby: In many women, *during total lactation, ovulation stops* and *menses do not take place*. During this period, a woman cannot conceive or has very low fertility. This method, too, is not hundred percent reliable as there are instances, despite lactation, the woman conceives even before menstruation restarts. *In some cases, menstruation and ovulation commence within three months*. The early restart of sex brings on quicker menstruation and ovulation due to hormonal effect on the system with breast milk decreasing.

Vasectomy and Tubectomy: Sterilising the male or the female is the best way for permanent stop to the birth of a child. In males, the operation is called *Vasectomy* in which the ducts (vas) carrying the sperms from the testes to the urethra in the penis is cut on both sides and tied beneath the skin of the scrotum. This operation is usually 100% successful. Vasectomy has no fears about loss of libido, difficulty to perform the sex act and general debilitating effects. *Vasectomy if performed unhygienically* can produce infection in the *internal genital organs*. In few cases, the operation causes *minor nerve pain during erection*. In female, the operation is known as *Tubectomy in which the fallopian tubes on either side are cut and ligatured*. The operation is performed easily, even a week after the delivery of a child when the uterus is still high up in position and the tubes are easy to ligature. The operation is performed by the *latest Laproscopy technique* by a pencil like instrument fitted with *microscope (microsurgery)* with hardly an inch long cut into the abdomen.

What is displacement of uterus?

The uterus or the womb is slung in the pelvic cavity and has sufficient movement in all directions. However, its natural position is upwards and forwards between the bladder and the rectum.

Displacement of uterus occurs because of several reasons, and is accompanied by *inflammation*. The downward displacement of uterus is known as *prolapse*. In this condition, the uterus slips downwards in the space between the bladder and the rectum. This condition is more common in overweight or too weak women.

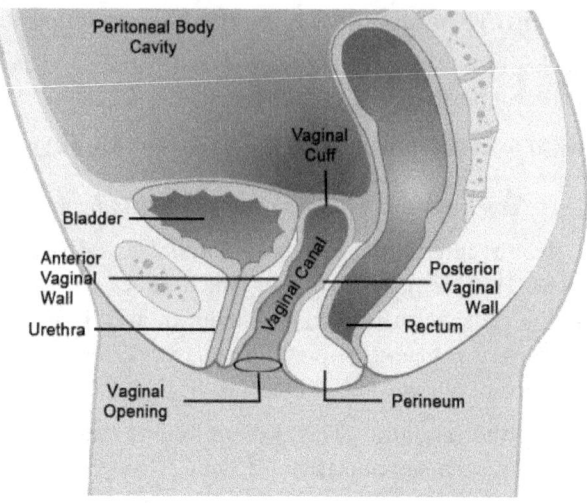

Displacement of Uterus

The displacement of uterus is frequent in women having repeated deliveries. The uterus gets distended during pregnancy when the foetus grows. The muscles supporting the uterus become too weak to bear the burden of the growing child in it. After the delivery of the child, the uterus and the surrounding muscles lack former shape and size. The symptom, which indicate displacement of the uterus include frequent backache, headache, heaviness in the bowels, external and internal muscles of the body become loose with feelings of depression. Doctors generally advise surgical interference for the treatment. Lack of proper exercise, acquisition of a coat of fat, deposition of morbid matter in the body and an inadequate diet lacking in essential vitamins and mineral substances can lead to weakness of the muscles of the body.

The following natural steps are recommended:
- ▶ Rest and relaxation in the bed and drain out tension from the body.
- ▶ Have a regular exercise plan designed to tone up the muscles supporting the uterus. Also seek advice of a naturopath doctor.
- ▶ Rub the parts immersed in water vigorously, while having a *Hip Bath*.
- ▶ Keep a hard pillow under the buttocks instead of under the head. This will help the uterus to return to its initial position.
- ▶ Lie on the floor with your knees touching your breast, which helps the uterus to resume to its normal position.
- ▶ Lie down after a meal with a pillow under your back. Have good diet containing enough fruits, milk or curd and green vegetables.

I suffer from premature ejaculation while having sex, please advise.

It is a malfunctioning due to psychological reasons, generally found in males and sometimes in females also, who are sexually more aroused than the opposite sex, who need a bit of foreplay to be ready for the intercourse. Too much anticipation of the sex act, too much of excitement can lead to premature ejaculation giving a feeling of failure or lack of fulfilment, which should follow the act of sexual intercourse. *The following are the natural ways to treat premature ejaculation:*
- ▶ Apply *Mud Pack on pubes* before sleep at night.

- *Kegal Exercise:* Squeeze the muscles in the anal area, as if you are trying to stop the flow of urine. This exercise strengthens the muscles of all the genital organs, the urethra (urinary tube) and the rectum. A regular practice will help you to control overejaculation.
- *Self-stimulation:* If you want to learn to slow your minutes' ejaculation reflex for four to six times during each session, masturbate three to four times a week, just bringing you close to orgasm but without ejaculating.
- *Scrotal Pull Technique:* During self-stimulation try practising to pull down on your scrotal sac before you reach the point of no return. During sex, you can do it yourself or seek the help of your partner.
- *Press the area on your perineum,* the space between the anus and the back of the scrotum, which stimulates the prostate – the gland that supplies the fluid for semen during ejaculation. Pressing on this spot when you are highly aroused helps block the ejaculatory reflex and can be quite pleasurable as well as it delays ejaculation. Press on it firmly and rhythmically at any point on the area during sex, after you have achieved a maximum erection.
- Mix in equal quantity seeds of 'Lajwanti' and sugar and take with milk in the morning.
- Avoid constipation and digestion disorders.

My husband suffers from impotency, How to increase his sex power?

Impotence (sexual weakness) is the inability to perform sex -- it may be *partial or complete, temporary or permanent.* Impotence can be in two categories: as a *result of organic reasons or psychological reasons.*

Organic impotence is caused due to disturbances of the endocrine glands (thyroid or pituitary glands), diseases of the central nervous system, severe disturbance of health and diabetes plays an adverse effect in this case. Deal with the disease that caused it and consult a physician.

Psychological impotence: This is caused by the factors like *ignorance about sex,* fear and *weakness or abnormality of sexual desire.* The psychological treatment of impotency is to find the true reason and realise what has caused it.

Treatment for impotency includes the following remedies:
- A healthy diet and exercise.
- A wet pack dipped in cold water on the spine can help the body to energise and strengthen the nervous system. Lie naked on the bed so that the wet bandage remains in constant touch with the spine.
- Drink plenty of water in a day to draw away all the morbid matter that has been poisoning the body system.

I am unable to satisfy my husband's sexual desire. Suggest remedies.

You suffer from frigidity: a condition in women, where she is unable to give herself sexually to the male partner and enjoy sex usually due to the following reasons, such as *psychological fear, wrong notions about sex, physical incapacity, hormonal and genital defects, cultural taboos* and *social position, intellectual upbringing and emotional status* playing a significant role in female *sexual behaviour, sexual indifferences* or *disliking for sex, physical causes,* such as *inflamed vagina,* a very rigid hymen, urinary problems or uterine infections and displaced ovaries.

My husband has a problem of involuntary discharge during sleep. Please advise.

Involuntary discharge of semen during sleep also known as *nocturnal emission* is one of the common disorders among youths or even in middle-aged persons. Night emission among youngsters is generally due to excitement because of reading vulgar literature or seeing a motion picture having exciting scenes. The following treatments are recommended to get rid of this psychological disorder:

- ▶ Avoid thoughts of sex
- ▶ Eat rich food
- ▶ Have dinner three hours before sleep
- ▶ Have evening walk followed by a bath
- ▶ Go to the bed early, not later than 9 p.m
- ▶ Application of a Mud Pack on pubes during sleep at night
- ▶ Hot and cold hip bath

Is excessive sex harmful?

There are women who are extremely passionate and feel uncontrollable sex desire. They are constantly attracted towards the opposite sex. This is often due to the following reasons:

- ▶ Deep sense of insecurity produced by neglect in childhood or adolescence.
- ▶ Genetically, some females are hyperfertile and highly sexual.

Excessively sexual women need *Psychotherapy*. *Hormone therapy* also neutralizes the effect of *estrogen* by administering *progesterone hormones.*

I feel unbearable pain during intercourse. Please advise.

The disorder is also known as *Dyspareunia*, which may arise from *muscular spasm of the vagina*. Sometimes, there is a superficial ulceration following some injury and tissues are painful to the touch. *Bladder infection* is common in such cases leading to further complications. Some of the causes of a painful intercourse are:

- ▶ Tightness in the female genital area after a surgery.
- ▶ Pelvic inflammation may cause pain during intercourse.
- ▶ Nervous tension due to unconsciously afraid of pregnancy.
- ▶ Problems like body odours, halitosis with the sex partner.
- ▶ Lack of understanding on the part of the male partner.
- ▶ May cause pain during marital relations.

I often feel urine escape, while laughing or carrying a load. Why so?

Disorder of leakage of urine, while laughing or carrying heavy luggage is generally due to weakness of *urethral opening or weak vaginal muscles*. It also happens sometimes as a result of *repeated childbirths and prolonged labour.* The overstretched urethral opening loses its *elasticity*. Sometimes, the urine escapes out with increased abdominal pressure due to short length of the urethra in females.

Is premarital sex harmful for an unmarried female?

Premarital sex is uncommon in Indian males and females due to early marriages. Sex life starts with marriage in most of the cases. Women feel the risk of pregnancy and avoid premarital sex in our country When a female goes through an abortion, it has physical risks to health and can produce haemorrhage, rupture of uterus, pelvic infection and other serious complications to catch pelvic infection including *vaginitis, urinary infection* and *risk of Sexually Transmitted Diseases* (STD).

I'm around 60. Is sex after menopause harmful?

Menopause is not the end of sex life and a woman can continue normal sex for years after she has stopped her periods. Many women enjoy satisfying sexual partnership even in old age. There are numerous couples in 70s to 80s who are involved in active sex life. Sometimes, menopausal women face problems having sex due to severe dryness of genital organs with pain during intercourse. *Lubricating creams* or *estrogen ointments* help to prevent this problem.

What are the common methods of family planning?

After marriage, a woman should know how to plan an ideal family and should be familiar with the various methods of family planning. Some of the prominent methods are *condoms for men, contraceptives for women,* use of diaphragm (rubber lid with a spring margin that closes the female cervix), cervical thimble-shaped cap (to be pushed into the vagina to cover the cervix), sponges and pessaries, *vaginal tablets and creams*, use of *intra-uterine device, intra-cervical device, vaginal rings, oral contraceptives and natural contraceptives.* Every newly married couple want to know about the *family planning techniques.* Birth control is important in cases when a woman is in a poor state of health and should control pregnancy until she is healthy enough to face the strain due to pregnancy and childbirth, when couples have a desire for children but want to space them out.

Following are various most widely used methods of birth control:

Abstinence: *This is basically the semen ejaculated near the entrance of the vagina without having had actual intercourse.* Care should be taken that the ejaculated semen may not come into contact with the *hymen* and gain access to the vagina reaching to the uterus.

Rhythm method: There is certain period every month when a woman is not likely to become pregnant. A woman in childbearing age sheds an egg from her ovary every month around the 14th day after the onset of her menstruation (with a regular 28 - day interval) between the menstrual periods. She might ovulate between the 12th to 16th days. Thus, a woman is more likely to become pregnant in case of sexual contact during this period. This method is about 85-90% effective.

Coitus interruptus: This is one of the oldest methods of birth control if the male partner has proper control over the withdrawal of his organ and the other partner has no objection to this practice, as some women reach a climax when their male partner ejaculates. It is not a 100% safe method of birth control.

Use of condoms: It is actually a thin latex sheath placed on the male organ to collect ejaculation of the semen. This is a frequently used safe method for birth control. The condom is discarded and thrown after single use. Many sex partners avoid using condoms due to decreased sensations when used, interrupted lovemaking when put on, may break while in use, may leak due to a manufacturing defect or expiry and may burst when in use or slip off after orgasm before removing.

Douches: Cleanse the vaginal canal using a syringe and stream of water. It is one of the poorest methods because it is not possible to flush out completely by douching and some of the sperms in the folds of the vagina may penetrate into the cervix.

Diaphragm: A circular rubber device that fits tightly in the vagina completely covering the cervix. The diaphragm can be inserted while standing or lying on the back or in sitting position as one sits for toilet by inserting fingers. The diaphragm is removed the next morning, or about five hours after termination of relations.

Contraceptive jellies, foams and creams: Highly effective products in destroying sperm within the vagina. These are inserted into the vagina an hour before the intercourse.

Intrauterine Devices (IUDs)

A plastic or plastic-metal object inserted by the gynaecologist into the uterine cavity. *It is a 98% effective device.* The device blocks the entrance of the sperm into the Fallopian Tube, where fertilization takes place. The device is usually changed after every three years. The device should be removed promptly in case the woman becomes pregnant.

Oral Contraceptives (Birth control pills)

The pills are taken orally, *which inhibit ovulation or formation of eggs.* These pills are 100% effective and should be taken strictly according to the advice of the doctor. Sometimes, complications like headache and nausea, weight gain, swelling and tenderness in breasts and inflammation of veins in legs arise while taking the birth control pills.

Why females menstruate?

Menstruation is a periodic change occurring in women consisting of discharge of blood from the cavity of the womb. It usually begins between 12 to 13 years in warm climatic regions and later in cold regions with duration varying usually from 3 to 7 days after an interval of 21 to 28 days. The menstrual flow stops when a woman becomes pregnant and stops completely at the age of about 50 or above. This period is known as *menopause*.

What are the common disorders of menstruation?

There are *two main disorders of menstruation:*

- ▶ *Absence of periods or scanty and painful discharge* known as *amenorrhoea* and *dismenorrhoea*.
- ▶ Profuse bleeding during periods known as *menorrhagia* or *irregular menstruation* called as *metrorrhagia*.

Amenorrhoe is a scanty discharge of menstrual blood or absence of menses flow may be due to :

- ▶ Anaemia
- ▶ Ill Health
- ▶ Disturbed nervous system
- ▶ Imperfect development or functioning of ovaries
- ▶ Inflammation of various internal organs (womb, ovaries or fallopian tubes).
- ▶ Serious or prolonged diseases like tuberculosis, aggravated dyspepsia, malaria, etc.
- ▶ Sudden fright or great grief, which may cause stoppage of the menstrual flow for

months. Seep 1 tablespoon each sesame seeds and small Caltrops (gokhru) in 200 ml water. Sweeten with sugar or honey and drink.
- ▶ Do not overstrain yourself mentally or physically.
- ▶ Hot and cold hip bath and sun-bathing will be beneficial.
- ▶ Fasting for 2 to 3 days during menstruation is advisable to provide physical, mental and psychological rest.
- ▶ A well-balanced food with restriction on salt is essential as water retention before, during and after menstruation is quite common.
- ▶ Drink plenty of coconut water, barley water, 'dhania' water or buttermilk, which have *diuretic effect*. Drink a glass of *warm water with honey* before going to bed, which relieves fatigue and induces sleep.

Dismenorrhoea have symptoms like pain during menstruation flow, vomiting sensation during periods and feeling of weakness, generally due to inflammation of internal organs, e.g. the womb, ovary defects or malfunctioning of the fallopian tubes.

The following herbal remedies are helpful to treat this *menstruation disorder*:
- ▶ The leaves of herbs, such as the Indian wild pepper (sambhalu), horse radish, (sahinjana), Indian lilac (bakayan), wild chicory (kasni), black night-shade (mako), marsh-mallow (khatmi), cotton plant (narma kapas) and dill (soya) are boiled in water.
- ▶ The leaves are cooked in sesame oil, dried and tied on the lower abdomen like a poultice.

Menorrhagia is the excessive discharge of blood from the womb during periods, usually due to *faulty functioning of the ovaries*. The following remedies help:
- ▶ *Amla* should be soaked in juice of green amla for three days and then ground into powder. Take this powder with milk.
- ▶ *A hot and cold Hip Bath is very beneficial for menorrhagia patients.*

Some women have heavy bleeding during menstruation and childbearing stage. Why?

There are several reasons for *excessive bleeding*, as detailed below:
- ▶ Heavy bleeding during the child-bearing age may be due to *miscarriage or abortion*, or as a result of an *ectopic pregnancy*. Tumour of uterus and cervix may result in *vaginal bleeding*. Women with irregular or very heavy bleeding should consult a doctor and have a *Pap test every six months*.
- ▶ A careful examination for the *presence of cancer* should be conducted by scrapping the inner lining of the uterus. Intermittent spotting may be due to *cervical polyp* – a common condition in women over 40. Heavy bleeding may be due to *fibroid tumours* and *polyps* within the uterus. In some cases, either the tumour or perhaps, the entire uterus may have to be removed.
- ▶ If a *woman is in mid-pregnancy and starts bleeding, she should be rushed to the doctor.* It may be too late to save the child in the womb. Severe blood loss may cause a danger to the life of the woman/or the mother in this condition.

- Heavy or painful bleeding is common in younger women due to various conditions, such as blood diseases, alcoholism, cirrhosis of the liver, vitamin B deficiency and abnormalities either in thyroid, pituitary or adrenal glands causing heavy bleeding. A complete medical examination including a careful evaluation of pelvic organs should be undertaken. In such cases, complete bed rest, a high protein diet and multi-vitamin capsules are recommended. If the woman has lost excess quantities of blood, a *transfusion may be needed*. Heavy bleeding following abortion usually requires a surgical operation to clean out from the uterus any fragments of the placenta still present in the uterus.
- During teenage, girls become depressed at the thought of painful periods, which is not abnormal and such girls should indulge in normal activities, as there is no reason for them to go to bed for two to three days every month due to this indisposition.
- During teenage years, young people suddenly become conscious of sex and striking changes take place within the body. Bad company and lack of proper guidance may lead to a life of sorrow and tragedy. A female should understand that her monthly cycle has a beneficial effect on her body. Menses may be irregular at first, but this is nothing to worry about. Some teenage girls have periods as early as 11 years of age, others do not begin until their 16 years, yet all are perfectly normal.

I am worried due to heavy, thick discharge. Kindly suggest what to do?

You are suffering from *Leucorrhoea* or *whites*, which is a symptom of many diseases peculiar to women. It consists of *white watery discharge* from the *uterus*, which may be thick consisting mainly of pus if the patient is suffering from a serious disorder of the genital organs.

Leucorrhoea discharge may be of several types, as below:
- In most cases, the discharge is catarrhal and chronic in nature.
- In few cases, the discharge follows or precedes the menstrual flow.
- In severe cases, the discharge continues throughout the intervening period.

The patients suffering from *leucorrhoea* have the following symptoms:
- Look pale and unhealthy.
- Feel tired at slight exertion.
- Have constant pain in the lower back.
- During early adolescence and teen years, increased white discharge combined with itching is common due to infection immediately before and after the periods.
- During the mid-cycle, white discharge increases when ovulation occurs.
- The discharge increases during pregnancy.
- During sexual excitement, there is excessive vaginal wetness.
- In anaemia and other general rundown states of health, the white discharge increases.
- Vaginal discharge and irritation increases because of bacterial or fungal infection due to *vaginitis*.
- There is always excessive vaginal discharge in ease-loving women, who neither do household work nor exercise their bodies. Manual workers are less susceptible to *leucorrhoea*.

The following remedies are suggested:

- ▶ Avoid wearing tight synthetic undergarments.
- ▶ Avoid use of strong antiseptics.
- ▶ Clean the genital parts once or twice a day to prevent infection.
- ▶ In case of husband having *urinary infection* or suffering from *trichomonasis or candidiasis*, he would have to be treated along with his wife, otherwise she would get re-infected repeatedly.
- ▶ Avoid highly spiced foods.
- ▶ Exercise the body by running, playing or involved in household work.
- ▶ Have sunbath daily for 15 to 20 minutes.
- ▶ Cold compress applied to the vagina helps a lot. A cold compress may be worn like a sanitary towel for an hour or may be worn during sleep.
- ▶ In young girls, the discharge may be due to *irritation of the labia or external genital organs, overactivity of sex glands and organs,* due to *soiled under garments, dirt and intestinal worms and masturbation.*
- ▶ In matured women, sometimes profuse yellowish discharge associated with urination may be due to *venereal diseases* (usually *gonorrhea*) or presence of creamy, slightly blood-stained discharge due to cancer in the uterus or cervix.

How to get rid of frequent gouts and leg cramps?

Gout is a type of arthritis causing throbbing pain that often strikes at night in pregnant women during the last trimester of pregnancy as well as during menopause. The skin turns red and hot, leaving the affected joint swollen and tender. Gout is caused by uric acid crystals, which settle in joints. Often the big toe is the prime target of its effect. Doctors usually inject toxic drugs for dissolving uric acid crystals or prescribe *ibuprofen* (800-milligrams) for relieving pain.

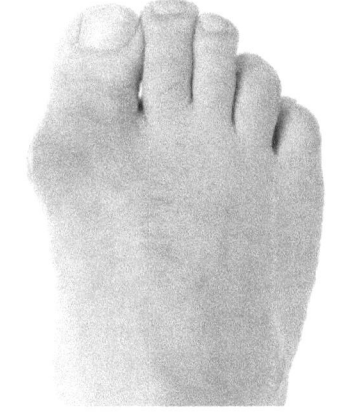

Gouts and Leg Cramps

The following curative measures are suggested to treat gout:

- ▶ *Apply crushed ice pack on the painful joint* for about 10 minutes.
- ▶ *Avoid taking high-purine foods* (high protein animal products, sweet bread, dry beans, whole-grain cereals and yeast) that contribute to *higher levels of uric acid.*
- ▶ Drink a lot of water to flush out excess uric acid from the body system.
- ▶ Avoid taking alcohol, which increases the uric acid production in the body that gets deposited on joints.
- ▶ *Eating cherries* prevents production of uric acid.
- ▶ *Vitamin B6* helps distribute water in the body to keep its tissues hydrated, which helps prevent uric acid from turning into crystals.
- ▶ *Taking a tablespoon of apple cider vinegar* in the morning daily.
- ▶ Mix charcoal into a bath and soak the affected foot in it for 30 to 60 minutes. Mix ½ cup of charcoal powder in water.

▶ Persons with high blood pressure should control their blood pressure by avoiding rich and spicy foods.

Leg cramps in the calves or feet commonly occur in women, especially in late pregnancy when she is resting or asleep. Cramps are usually caused by factors, such as *fatigue in calf muscles, pressure on the nerves to the legs*, impaired circulation and calcium-phosphorus imbalance in the blood.

Cramps are relieved by the following measures:
▶ The muscle is slowly and gently stretched.
▶ Gently stretch the calf muscles. Keep the knees straight, ankles bent and heels resting on the floor. When the leg cramp is severe, seek help.
▶ A foot cramp, which usually tightens the muscles of the arch and curls the toes. Relief is brought by stretching out the toes. Avoid curl on your toes.

What is menopause?

A female becomes reproductive in her early teens and can bear a child till her mid or late-forties. After passing through various stages of her sex life, a woman enters menopause, which marks the end of her fertile period and the beginning of a new phase. When periods finally stop and fertility ceases, menopause sets in. At the beginning of menopause, the usual complaints include *hot flushes, dizziness* and *fainting, lack of energy* and *depression, fainting, burning feet* and *hands, vaginal dryness, loss of sleep, severe itching, facial hair growth, sudden increase in weight, mental tension, high blood pressure, complete loss of interest in sex, palpitations, chilly feeling* and *constant backache arising from low levels of estrogen in the blood stream* and *imbalanced hormonal levels.*

Menopause-usually occurs around the age of 50 and is called the **'The Change'** when functioning of the of ovaries produce eggs, the swelling and bursting of the egg or the sac takes place, release of the hormones (*estrogen secretion*), *monthly menstrual shedding of uterine cells and blood becomes irregular* and slowly *comes to a halt*. The prominent symptoms during menopause include *hot flashes and sudden chills, lowered sexual* desire, *emotionally upset, insomnia, depression, memory loss* and *sudden change in the moods along with night sweating*. Sometimes, the sweating is so high that you may have to change the bedsheet.

The following measures are advised during menopause:
▶ Make life an adventure. Find a new hobby and change in the career.
▶ Daily exercise should be a part of your daily life. Walking, jogging, bicycling, jumping rope dancing, swimming or any other *daily exercise can relieve menopausal disorders. Yoga aids relaxation and reduces stress.*
▶ *Hot flashes are body's response to lower estrogen levels and more than 75% women usually have hot flashes lasting between two to three minutes.* During excretion of hot flashes, heat is produced in the body, the face reddens and there *is excessive sweating.*
▶ Nutrients can help control or completely eliminate hot flashes. *Vitamin A is as effective as estrogen* (recommended daily dose 400 to 1200 international units, as recommended

Important Facts Prior to Conception

by your doctor). In case of night sweats, have two doses during the night as per suggestions of your doctor.
- Vitamin E helps in case of *vaginal dryness*.
- *Learn meditation or yoga or sit quietly*, eyes closed to relax your mind.
- *Alcohol triggers hot flashes. Similarly, cut down caffeine containing beverages* that stimulate production of the stress hormones and trigger hot flashes.
- *Wear fibre clothes*. Synthetic fibre trap heat and produce perspiration during a hot flash.
- Drink a lot of water or juice, especially after exercising to check the body temperature.
- Eat small meals-*minimum three meals a day*. Even five to six small meals a day will help your body regulate the temperature more easily.
- *Vitamin B complex helps to reduce stress in menopausal women.*
- The herb, 'sage' works very well if menopausal woman have hot flashes throughout the day and sweat during night. Drink a *sage tea*.
- *Hydrotherapy treatment* is very helpful *for menopausal women*. The body expels toxins during menstruation. When the menstrual cycle decreases or stops, the body requires another outlet for the toxins, so it starts *sweating or has hot flashes*. It is advised to have *sauna (steam) bath* to release the toxins from the body. In case, a sauna or steam room is not possible, take a *hot bath for 10-20 minutes a day*.
- *Valerian* and *lavender* herbs help better sleep. Take 300 to 500 milligrams *Valerian extract one hour before retiring to bed* at night. Dabbing a few drops of Lavender essential oil on your pillow before sleep can help you to get a sound sleep.
- *Acupressure therapy relieves insomnia and anxiety* in menopausal women. Stimulate two pressure points on the feet for 1 to 3 minutes each with your middle and index fingers.
- Women passing through their menopausal period if stay sexy and have regular intercourse once a week, or once a fortnight have few or no hot flashes or night sweating as compared to those women who don't indulge in sexual intercourse at all. *Having frequent sex helps moderate drop in estrogen levels, which reduces hot flashes. A study reveals that regular sexual activity stimulates the functioning of the ovaries.*
- Vaginal dryness from a lack of estrogen *decreases* interest in sexual intercourse among menopausal women. Lubricants suitable for vaginal dryness include vaginal jelly, vegetable oil and unscented cream or oil.
- *Vitamin E can be used to massage as a lubricant*. Break open Vitamin E capsules and mix to the lubricant.

Doctor says, I am suffering from Anaemia. How to get relief or cure anaemia?

Anaemia is iron deficiency in the body common among women. It is a condition in which *the blood has less red cells*, which results in *lesser supply of oxygen* to the tissues resulting in *weakness, lassitude and pallor. Iron-deficiency anaemia* may cause symptoms such as *dizziness, loss of appetite, diarrhoea, abdominal pain, pale complexion, palpitation of the heart, shortness of breath, feeling of weakness and frequent headaches,* etc. The blood needs iron to produce

Red Blood Cells (RBCs). Women who don't get enough iron in their diets, or who have heavy menstrual periods may have insufficient levels of either **Red Blood Cells** or **Haemoglobin**. Women whose haamoglobin level decline feel tired and weak. If you have excessively heavy or lengthy menstrual flow, or *your menstrual period lasts for more than seven days, consult a doctor immediately.* If you are having *rectal bleeding, you need to see a doctor again.* Improve diet and keep your lifestyle in order to have a healthy baby and trouble-free delivery of child.

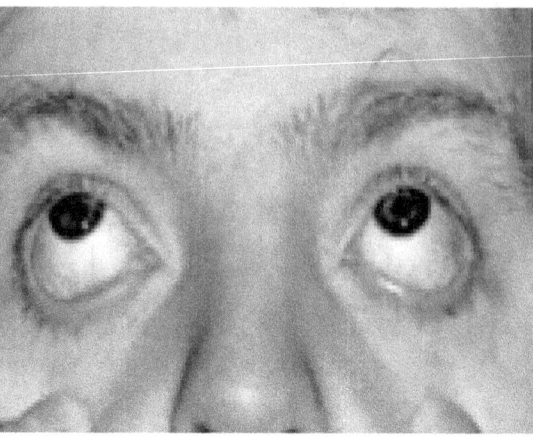
Anaemia

Here are a few remedies for anaemic women:

- *Have iron-rich food.* Good sources of iron include *whole grains*, such as *barley and oats, beans and peas, seeds and nuts, fruits and vegetables.*
- *Calcium rich foods* put more iron in your body. Dairy products decrease iron absorption in women with anaemia, whereas increase your intake of beans, peas, *soabeans*, sesame seeds, soups and leafy green vegetables increases the iron content in the body. *Inadequate diet is one of the most common causes of anaemia.*
- *Vitamin C is acidic and helps the body to absorb the iron contents.* Squeeze the juice of a lemon into a glass of water and drink before meals.
- Alcoholic beverages deplete the body of vitamin B complex and minerals, which worsen anaemia. *Reduce sugar intake*, which also depletes the body of vitamin B complex.
- *Delete caffeine products like coffee, black tea, soda, chocolate, etc.* from *your daily diet*, which depletes the body of vitamin B complex.
- If *anaemia results from iron deficiency, iron pills are suggested.* But if anaemia is associated with *Vitamin B-12 deficiency,* the vitamin must be administered by *injections.*

Chapter - 2

First Trimester of Pregnancy

First Trimester

The first trimester of pregnancy lasts for *three and a half months or 14 weeks*. During this stage of pregnancy, you may experience the dreaded *morning sickness* (which can occur anytime during the day and *sore and enlarged breasts*. During this stage, it's vital that you get enough vitamins, minerals and nutrients as they are essential for growth and development. It's a good idea to consult with your healthcare provider to determine what is best for you.

Nutrition and Exercise

- 2200 calories/day
- Well balanced, healthy diet with adequate fibre promotes baby's growth and mother's energy and comfort
- Take prenatal vitamins, as prescribed
- Avoid the use of alcohol and tobacco
- Small, more frequent meals may help a nauseous woman get good nutrition
- Many women can continue to exercise regularly
- Daily exercise that suits your level of fitness can help decrease fatigue and stress
- Discuss your exercise habits with your healthcare provider
- Avoid overheating and maintain good hydration during exercise

I am not having periods since the past ten/days or monthe. What are the important signs of pregnancy?

The following symptoms are observed when pregnancy develops:

- Missed period is one of the common cause for developing pregnancy, but sometimes the pregnant woman keeps having periods, two to three months after conceiving.
- Nausea and vomiting after three weeks, but many times, a conceived woman does not have nausea or vomiting.
- Exhaustion, tiredness and excessive giddiness are few symptoms.
- Morning sickness.

Motherhood ....Through a Year of Pregnancy

- ▶ Change of taste and strong likings and dislikings for certain foods.
- ▶ Frequent urge to urinate.
- ▶ Engorged and tender breasts.
- ▶ Increased discharge from nipples.
- ▶ Increased vaginal discharge in most cases.

I am 20 years old and just married. I have missed my periods and want to be sure whether I am pregnant or not. What do you recommend?

Pregnancy test kits are available over the counter and are very simple to use. You could get one and test your *morning urine sample for pregnancy*. If the card shows *two lines, you are pregnant,* if only *one line,* then you could have *missed your periods* due to some other reasons like *hormonal disorder*, which can be rectified by simple medications.

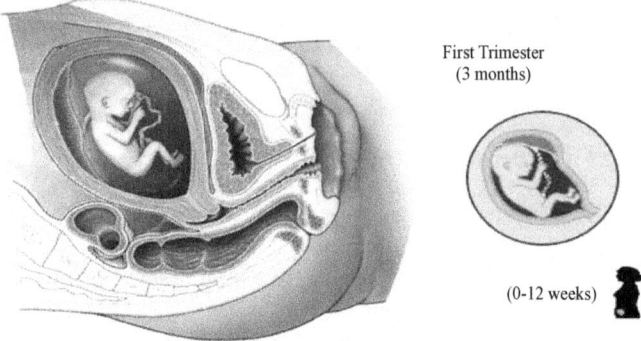

First Trimester of Pregnancy

What are the prominent developments of baby during the first trimester of pregnancy?

- ▶ After conceiving, the fertilized egg travels down the fallopian tube to get embedded in the lining of the womb in the 3rd week.
- ▶ By the 6th week, the embryo is 1.25 cm long, but doesn't look like a baby. It has a large head with pits for eyes and a tail.
- ▶ By the 12th week, the baby measures about 9 cm and weighs approximately 9 gm appearing like a *human embryo* with *all internal organs*.

Remember, the foetus *takes nutrition from the mother* and *discharges its waste material* into the blood through the *placenta*. Always take medicines as prescribed by a doctor. The placenta also produces hormones necessary during pregnancy. *After the baby's birth, the placenta gets separated from the uterine wall and is expelled out from the uterus.*

How to diagnose pregnancy?

Radiological diagnosis of pregnancy is a widely used method for the diagnosis of pregnancy. Radiography is done to find out the position of the foetus, its presentation and position, maturity, structural abnormalities and multiple pregnancy including the intra-uterine death. Radiological method of diagnosis should not be employed before the 28th week. To find out a multiple pregnancy, find out the view of the pelvic by X-ray centred above the pelvis, so that the central ray of the X-ray beam passes through about three inches behind the anterior border of the pubis. *Pregnancy can also be diagnosed by inserting hand into the vagina and check the foetus.*

First Trimester of Pregnancy

What are the various types of deliveries?

Fertilization is the union of a mature ovum with a sperm. If sexual intercourse takes place within 12 to 24 hours of ovulation, then one of the thousands of sperms deposited in the vagina unites with the ovum to fertilize it after traveling through the uterine cavity and reach the fallopian tube. The fertilized ovum gradually grows into the foetus and it takes about *266 days for a fertilized egg to grow into a baby.*

The various types of deliveries are as follows:

Normal Vaginal Delivery: The child is delivered in normal ways but sometimes aided with a small cut at the vaginal outlet. The process in known as *Episiotomy* and is done to help

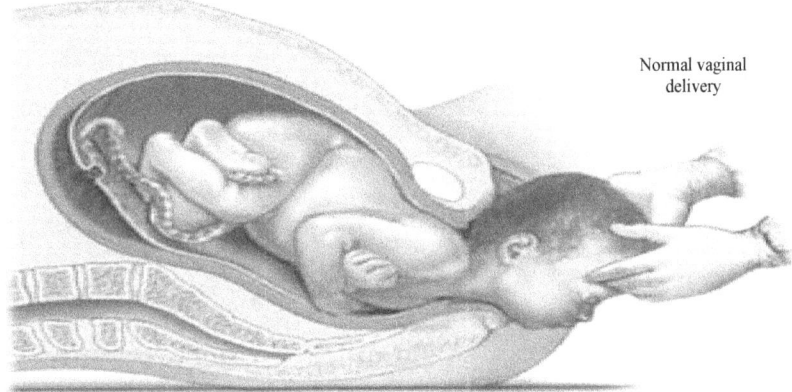

Normal Vaginal Delivery

quicker delivery with undue downward pressure on the uterus and adjoining parts of the bladder and the rectum.

Suction Delivery: A process in which suction is applied to the low descending head of the baby to hasten deliver. It is also called the *vacuum method of delivery and helps the mother to deliver quickly. Anaesthesia is not required in most of the cases.*

Forcep Delivery: This is a case in which the baby's head is helped out with the use of forceps, e.g. a large pair of tongs, which grasp the baby's head for applying a downward pull. Mild anaesthesia is given to the mother to avoid excessive pain. In case of *forcep delivery*, the

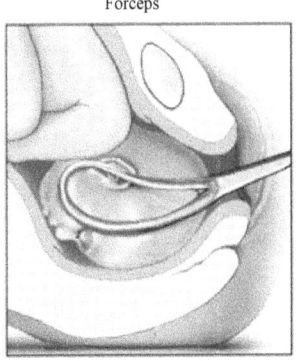
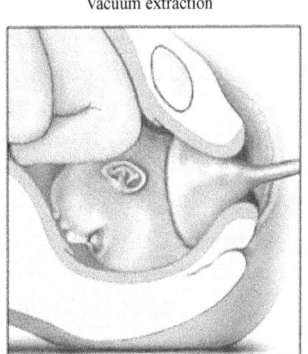

Suction Delivery & Forcep Delivery

membranes must be ruptured and the bladder and *the rectum should be emptied.* Risks in case of a forcep delivery includes injuries to the soft vaginal passages due to carelessness in application of the blades or by too rapid extraction, which may *cause haemorrhage or injuries to the child* like fractures of the skull, intra-cranial haemorrhage, injury to the eyes, facial paralysis and compression of the head.

Multiple Pregnancy: If you have any history of *multiple births in the family,* tell your doctor to diagnose seriously. It can be diagnosed by the size of the womb or pelvic examination or USC scanning of the abdomen.

In case of signs of a multiple pregnancy, visit your doctor more frequently and have complete rest between the 30th to the 37th weeks, to avoid premature delivery and sometimes possibility of a *caesarean section.* It requires highly skilled pediatric care.

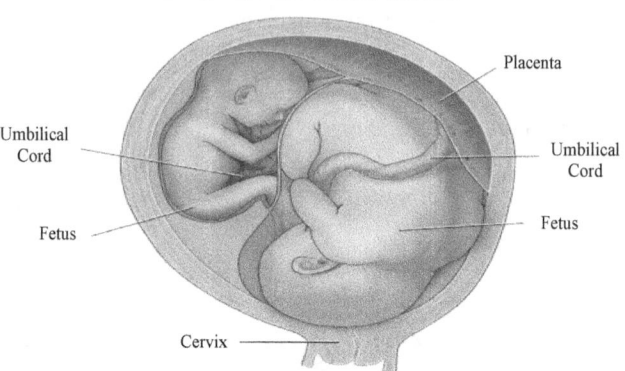

Multiple Pregnancy

Ectopic or Tubal Delivery: It is a rare complication in which the fertilized ovum or embryo becomes blocked in its passage through the fallopian tube. Sometimes, the embryo continues to grow as it normally would within the uterus.

However, the space between the tubes is too small to allow expansion, and that may rupture causing a *serious haemorrhage* and *intense pain in the pelvis.* Consult your doctor for *necessary surgery* as soon as a *tubal pregnancy* is suspected. Ectopic pregnancy causes *maternal death, pain, heavy vaginal bleeding,* etc.

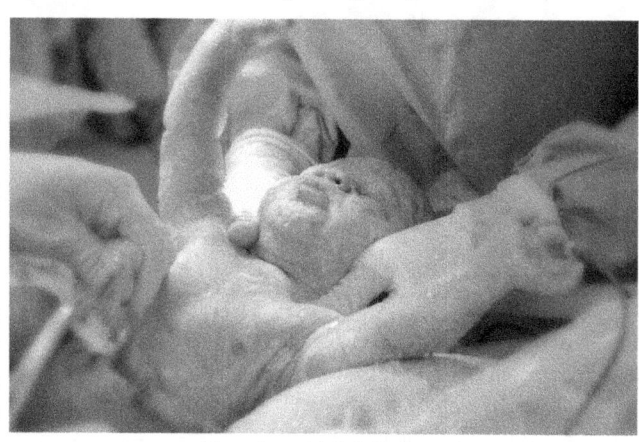

Ectopic or Tubal Delivery

Induced Delivery: In this case, labour is brought on or induced artificially by *rupturing the membranes and letting out a little amniotic fluid, which stimulates labour pains.* When the pain are too feeble or the delivery is overdue, labour is induced by administrating medicines, which contract the uterus.

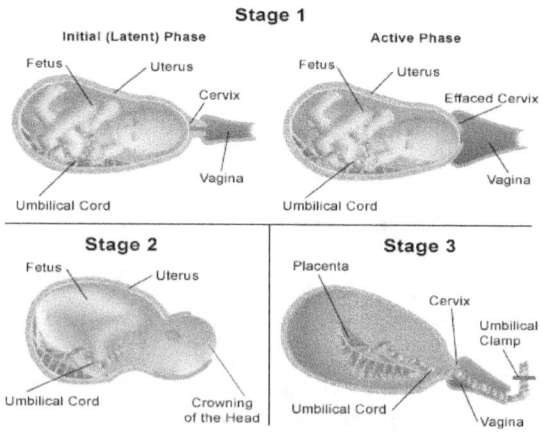

Induced Delivery

First Trimester of Pregnancy

Premature Delivery: The termination of pregnancy after the foetus is called *premature birth* or the foetus is born dead, it is *stillbirth*. Premature delivery is usually the problem with the placenta, faulty blood supply to the foetus, defective hormone production and effect of injurious toxins and chemicals through the blood to the foetus. *Premature deliveries* include *obliquity of the uterus, uterus subseptus, premature foetus, dead foetus, hydramnois, placenta praevia and pelvic tumour.*

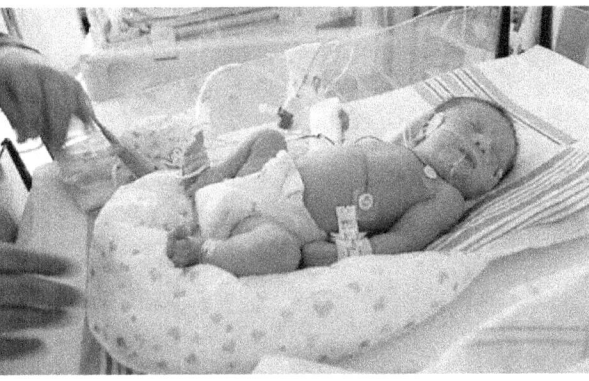
Premature Delivery

Breech Delivery: Most babies are born with the head first position instead of the feet first the or shoulder first. If the birth canal is adequate and the baby is small, there may not be any serious difficulty because of breech position. If the unborn baby is bulky and the birth outlet is small, this could be dangerous to both the mother and the baby. Avoid travelling or bulky jerks during the last few days.

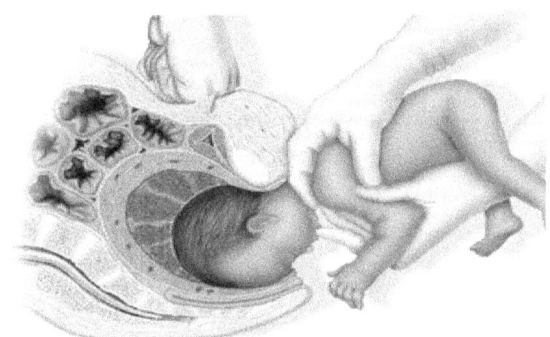
Infant's head caught in the birth canal during breech delivery
Breech Delivery

An expectant mother should ensure the following care:

- ▶ The abdominal and uterine walls must be relaxed.
- ▶ An anesthesia should always be given, if necessary.
- ▶ The cervix must be dilated sufficiently to admit the entire hand in uterus.
- ▶ The position of the foetus must have been exactly mapped out before the hand is introduced in the uterus.
- ▶ The vulva and the vagina must be thoroughly cleansed.
- ▶ Sterile rubber gloves should be worn.
- ▶ Pass the hand into the uterus in cone-shape.
- ▶ The patient should be placed on her side or on her back.
- ▶ The head must be pushed up into the fundus of the uterus by an external hand.

Sometimes, I feel the uterus is pushing outwards, why so?

Probably, you suffer from *displacement of the uterus*. Generally, the enlargement of uterus and abdomen occur due to pregnancy and *large tumour, hydramnios* and *multiple pregnancy*. You must consult a lady doctor immediately. It may be the *displacement of the uterus*. Remember, *the bladder must be carefully emptied by the catheter before examination.*

The displacement of the uterus must be treated by the following ways:

- ▶ If by the 12th week, the uterus is still retroverted, then a large *ring pessary* is inserted into the vagina.
- ▶ The patient should lie in the semi-prone position and remain in bed for a couple of days in the Sim's Position.
- ▶ The pessary should be left in the vagina until after the 16th week of pregnancy under doctor's supervision.
- ▶ If the uterus remains retroverted after 48 hours, then *manual reposition of the uterus may be undertaken*. Simple manual reposition is done by inserting two fingers in the posterior fornix and pushing the fundus upwards and forwards. The cervix is then caught backwards by one finger and the other hand on the abdomen to catch the fundus.
- ▶ After the uterus has been replaced, a large ring pessary should be inserted and not removed until after the 16th week of pregnancy.
- ▶ In case of a patient with a history of previous abortions, a *laprotomy* should be done immediately.

What are some of the common abnormalities of the uterus?

There are several types of major developmental abnormalities of the uterus given below in which you should seek advice of your doctor such as:

1. Uterus didelphys (*complete duplication of the uterus, cervix and vagina*).
2. Uterus bicornis bicollis
3. Uterus bicornis unicollis
4. Uterus bicornis unicollis (with one horn rudimentary)

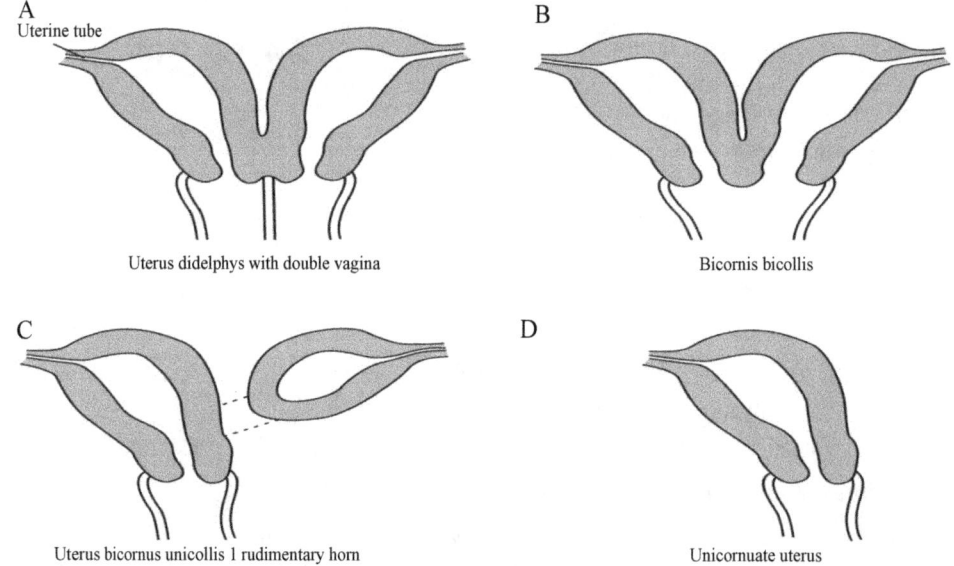

Abnormalities of the Uterus

First Trimester of Pregnancy

1. Uterus septus
2. Uterus subseptus
3. Uterus arcuatus
4. Uterus unicorni

What are the physical examinations during pregnancy?

Tell your doctor regarding the *difficulty in previous delivery if any, abortions* or *miscarriages* (if any) in the past, the birth of premature or macerated foetuses or death of children occurring in early infancy (if any), type of blood of both parents, your present health problems, existence of cardiac or pulmonary disease or toxaemia, breathlessness, palpitation, cough, excessive vomiting, persistent headaches, swelling of the hands or face, diminished amount of urine, dimness of vision, condition of the bowels, the presence of vaginal discharges and their nature, swelling of the feet or legs, presence of haemorrhoids or varicose veins, etc.

After preliminary questioning, usually the doctor asks the patient to undress and lie upon an examination couch to have a general survey of the *circulatory, respiratory* and the *digestive* system. See that the doctor inspects the breast noting their development, the condition of *nipples*, *areola* (the darkish part around the nipples) and the presence as well as the amount of secretion from them. (if any). The blood pressure should be estimated frequently. The patient's height is recorded and it may be worthwhile to mention that women of short stature below five feet are more likely to have *small pelvis* than *taller women*. The patient's weight is noted and a check on weight gain is made on every visit to the doctor during the pregnancy period.

Abdominal examination is another important step by the doctor. In early pregnancy, the doctors note down the size of the uterus and exclude any morbid abdominal conditions. Prior to the 26th week of pregnancy, abdominal diagnosis of presentation and position is often inaccurate. The level of the fundus, the presence of uterine soufflé, and hearing the heart beat should be examined. At the 38th week, a final review is carried out and relationship of the foetal head to the maternal pelvis is determined. A study is be made to determine the size of the head related to the pelvis brim.

Pelvic examination is done to investigate the condition of the pelvic organs and to estimate the size and shape of the pelvic canal. It is necessary to measure the pelvis by your doctor by means of a *bimanual examination* to diagnose that pregnancy is confirmed and determine the presence or absence of *pelvic swellings,* such as *uterine fibroids* or *ovarian cysts*. There are *three methods* of *pelvic examination*:

▶ **External Examination:** The measurements are made with a pair of *calipers* to find out any deformity.

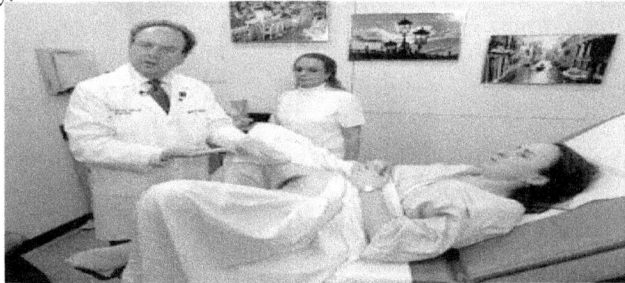

External Examination

- ▶ **Internal Examination:** Interspinous diameter is measured with calipers. The two anterior-superior spines are located, where the points of caliper are placed on their outer lips and the measurement read off. Normally, it should be 9-1/2 to 10 inches (24 –25 cm.). The Intercristal diameter is also measured at the points passed slowly around the *iliac cresta* until the points of greatest separation are found when the measurement is read normally, which should be 10-1/2 to 11 inches (26-27 cm.).

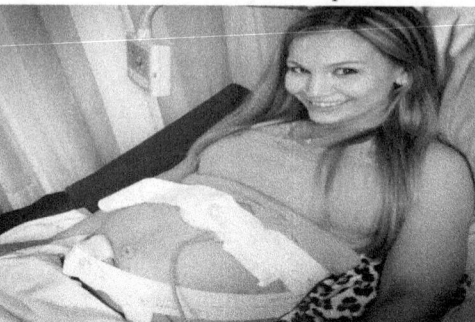

Internal Examination

- ▶ **By X-rays:** The size of the pelvis and the foetal head can be assessed by X-rays. This process is known as *Radiographic Pelvimetry*.

The blood pressure of the patient should be ascertained at each visit to the doctor. The blood pressure should not rise above 140/90. During the *middle trimester of pregnancy*, the blood pressure is often low and the reading of 110/70 may be recorded.

Urine and haemoglobin should be checked once a month during pregnancy. Usually, the patient is asked to pass water before she undresses for the physical examination. Examination of urine is most important throughout pregnancy to check the *presence of albumin, presence of sugar, pus and other abnormalities*. Urine should be examined once a month in the first six months, thereafter more frequently as pregnancy advances. If the albumin is present in the urine along with a vaginal discharge, a mid-stream specimen of urine should be obtained and a doctor should be consulted.

The *haemoglobin should be checked throughout pregnancy.* If you are suffering from anaemia, there is plenty of time to correct this. All Rh Negative patients have their blood examined for the presence of antibodies at regular intervals.

Be careful when the weight increases during pregnancy. In normal pregnancy, the increase in weight begins with the 4th month and continues at an average rate of about *2 kg per month* to about the 39th week, and the total weight gain being about *12 kg. An abnormal gain in weight should be informed to your doctor.*

Remember, the vaginal secretion in a healthy pregnancy differs only in its increased quantity from that of a healthy non-pregnant woman. It is *whitish in colour, containing epithelial cells, leucocytes* and *mucus*. It contains large '*vaginal bacilli*'.

What is the correct way to clean the genitals due to frequent discharge during the period of pregnancy?

The birth canal can be divided into *three parts:*
- ▶ The *vulva*, which may be designated as the *septic tract*.
- ▶ The vaginal area has *acidic secretions, fungi* and *leucocytes*.
- ▶ The cavity of the uterus, separated by the plug of the mucus from the vagina, is entirely devoid of any form of organism.

Prior to delivery, a thorough cleansing is must. For cleansing of the vulva, the patient should have a complete bath at the very commencement of labour, and the nurse should see that the rectum and the bladder are emptied. It is usually suggested that the patient should be given an *enema* in every case, irrespective of whether the bowels have acted naturally or not, unless the patient is in strong labour when the nurse arrives. The nurse should then pay special attention to the genitals. The hair should be shaved. Before a vaginal examination is made, the vulva is swabbed with an antiseptic solution. The *labia minora* must be separated and wiped with *pledgets of wool soaked* in an antiseptic solution always be drawn from being backwards to prevent carrying forward any septic matter from near the anus.

What is the right way for vaginal examination by the doctor, I was told that sometimes it causes infections?

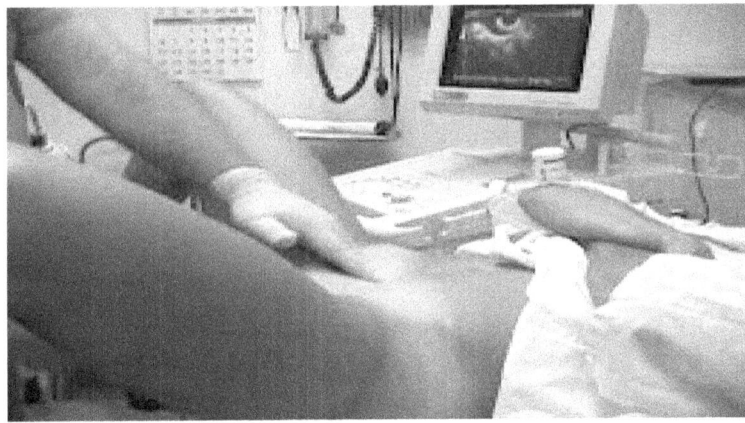

Vaginal Examination

The use of *abdominal palpation* has been recommended. Where a vaginal examination is necessary, it must be done with care. The patient should be on her back rather than on her side, so as to diminish the risk of the hand coming into contact with the anus. Cleanse your hands and vulva before conducting the examination. The *labia minora* is separated apart by the left hand fingers. The fingers of the right hand are introduced in the vagina without coming into contact with the vulva at all, or at least only the inner surfaces of the labia minora, which have also been cleansed. In case, the patient is passing through the stage of labour, it is well to introduce the fingers into the vagina during a pain and prolong the examination until it passes off.

The doctor ascertains the following points during vaginal examination:

   1. The state of labour; how far advanced it is?

   2. Presentation and position?

   3. Are the membranes ruptured? (be careful not to rupture the same).

   4. The state of vagina and perineum to check rigidity, moistness or dryness.

   5. Is the pelvis normal?

   6. Is the cord prolapsed?

What are embryo changes during the approximate nine months of pregnancy?

The delivery date is generally 280 days after the first day of the last period.

The 40-week period of pregnancy is classified into three trimesters, as mentioned below:

▶ The first trimester period begins from the 1st to the 12th week.
▶ The second trimester starts from the 13th week till the 28th week.
▶ The third trimester begins from the 29th to the 40th week.

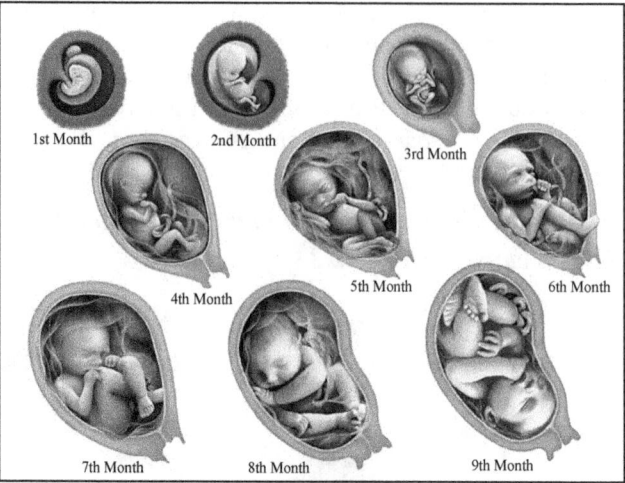

Embryo Changes

The child in womb becomes theoretically capable of living a separate individual life in about the 28th week of pregnancy. It is important to know the age of a foetus or embryo, both for clinical and medical reasons.

At the end of the 4th week: The embryo is much curved, head and tail being close together. It measures from 2.5 to 4 mm. from the crown to rump. The brain and the cord are enclosed, eye and ear vesicles are visible. The heart is prominent and is beginning to divide in to four chambers.

At the end of the 8th week: The embryo is about an inch (25 mm.) long in crown rump measurement. The head has a human shape, whereas, the tail has nearly disappeared. The hands and feet begin to appear. Eyes, nose and ears are recognizable. The external genitals are visible, but the sex is not distinguishable. The *embryo now becomes the foetus.*

At the end of the 12th week: The foetus is about 3-1/2 to 4 inches long weighing about 50 gm. The intestines are enclosed in the abdomen and the umbilical cord is beginning to show spiral turns. *Sex can be determined by the presence or absence of the uterus.* Most of the bones begin to show the centre of ossification.

At the end of the 16th week: The foetus is about six inches (15 cm.) long and weighs about 190 gm. Sex is clearly defined at this stage. The fine downy hair starts appearing on the skin.

At the end of the 20th week: The foetus is about 7 to 8 inches (18-20 cm.) long weighing about 450 gm. The head is still relatively large. The cord is about 12 inches long.

At the end of the 24th week: The foetus is about 9 inches (23 cm.) long and weighs about 930 gm. Fat begins to deposit under the skin. Hair appears on the head.

At the end of the 28th week: The foetus is about eleven inches (28 cm.) long weighing about 1300 gm. *The eyelids are now open and the papillary membrane starts disappearing.* The body is now covered with fine hair (lanugo). The intestines contain a dark green tarry matter known as the *meconium. A child born at this time very seldom survives.*

At the end of the 32nd week: The foetus is nearly 12 inches long weighing about 2075 gm. The hair on the scalp is thicker.

At the end of the 36th week: The length of the foetus is nearly 14 inches weighing about 2500 gm. The subcutaneous fat has increased, and the face is less wrinkled with the body more round. *A child born at this time has a very fair chance of survival.*

At the end of the 40th week: The total length reaches 20 inches weighing about 3200 gm. The fingers have complete nails and the skin is pink and smooth. The diameter of the head becomes normal. *In the male, the testicles are in the scrotum.*

I am not having periods which were due two weeks ago, should I visit a doctor for examinations?

The following tests and examinations are performed at the first prenatal visit to a doctor, which helps assure the birth of a healthy baby:

- A complete medical history and physical examination.
- A pelvic examination to confirm *pregnancy*, estimate the *size and shape of your pelvis, to do a Pap smear to detect cervical cancer* and to test for syphilis or gonorrhoea.
- Blood test to determine your blood type, Rh factor, test for anaemia, infection, syphilis and German measles immunity.
- Urine test to check protein, sugar and any infection.
- At each prenatal monthly visit to your doctor, check up for your *weight, blood pressure, urine* and *abdominal examination* to measure the growth of the uterus, the foetus and estimate the size and position of the foetus.

On finding the symptoms of pregnancy, the pregnant woman should consult a doctor and tell him/her the following:

- The date of the first day of the last menstruation period.
- The duration and heaviness in the menstrual flow in past.
- Any complication faced in previous pregnancies.
- The number of children and their usual weight at the time of birth in previous cases of pregnancy.
- The duration of lactation (breast feeding) in the past cases.
- The number of years of marriage and the number of children.
- Any miscarriage or termination of pregnancy that took place in the past.
- If undergoing any treatment at the present or in the past. Also in case of a past surgery, inform the doctor.
- The past history of health with details of prolonged suffering, such as *diabetes, high blood pressure, epilepsy or heart disease.*
- If you or your husband or any close blood relation is suffering from a hereditary or venereal disease.
- If ever exposed to X-rays.
- If you are anaemic.

- ▶ If suffering from *cystitis* (painful and embarrassing condition in which there is a frequent urge to urinate.
- ▶ Any abnormal condition, such as frequent pain in the abdomen or pelvic region, blood discharge, and white discharge accompanied with mucus. Boils or itching around urinary opening, pain during intercourse, irregular menses or any other condition.

What are some of the important monthly examinations required for a pregnant woman?

A pregnant woman must undergo the following monthly tests/examinations by the doctor:

- ▶ Weight gain.
- ▶ Recording blood pressure.
- ▶ Oral hygiene checked regularly.
- ▶ Signs of anaemia, swelling of legs, feet and hands.
- ▶ Inspection of heart and lungs.
- ▶ Examination of breasts to check for any lumps and abnormality of nipples.
- ▶ Vaginal examination. During the first 12 weeks, the uterus cannot be felt by placing hand on the abdomen. To confirm pregnancy, an internal pelvic examination has to be performed between the 6th and the 10th week of pregnancy.

To find a correct picture and determine the size of the uterus, a gynaecologist gently inserts two gloved fingers into the vagina and pushes firmly on the abdomen to assess the uterus thoroughly. The patient is made to lie flat on the examination table bending legs in such a way so as to keep the feet on the table and the pelvic muscles relaxed.

What is to be avoided during the first trimester of pregnancy?

A pregnant woman should avoid the following during the first trimester:

- ▶ Wearing tight clothes
- ▶ Drinking excessive tea and coffee
- ▶ Jerky or long travelling
- ▶ Overexertion
- ▶ X-rays
- ▶ Strong medicines without doctor's prescription
- ▶ Smoking or drinking
- ▶ Standing for a long time or getting up suddenly from the sitting position.
- ▶ Contact with animals, especially cats and birds, which may lead to abortion, premature delivery or birth of a sickly baby.
- ▶ Not consulting the doctor on finding symptoms, such as bleeding or excessive discharge through vagina, abdominal pain, painful burning urination, persistent vomiting, frequent fever and feeling of dizziness. If you feel dizzy, sit down with your head between your toes.

What precautions should be taken during the first trimester of pregnancy?

A pregnant woman should take the following precautions during the first trimester of pregnancy:

- ▶ A monthly check up and consultation with the doctor.

First Trimester of Pregnancy

- Have frequent small meals – about 6 to 7 times a day.
- Get 8 to 10 hours sleep during night and minimum 1 to 2 hours rest during the day.
- Restrict fluid intake in the evening to avoid frequent urination during night.
- Hormonal changes lead to a feeling of *lethargy and exhaustion during the first trimester of pregnancy*. So a complete rest is essential during this period.
- Consult a doctor in case of a burning sensation while passing urine.
- Eat hygienically cooked food.
- Relax for few minutes with your feet up during the lunch hours.
- Take anti-vomiting drug in consultation with the doctor in case of severe nausea and vomiting.

The pregnancy calendar during the first trimester of pregnancy:

Foetal growth during the first trimester:

- After conception, up to four weeks, the foetal length is about-1/4th inches and during this period the eyes, ears, mouth, brain, spine, spinal cord and the umbilical cord start forming.
- The heart starts beating by the 25th day. It is called the *ovum* until two weeks. By the end of the 8th week, the length of the foetal grows up to 1-1/8 inches with the formation of arms, legs, bones, internal organs, the brain and the tooth buds. It is called the **embryo**.
- By the end of 12 weeks, the foetal growth reaches to 3 inches long when the movement of arms and legs begins, the fingers and the toes are formed. Sex is distinguishable in this stage. The foetus may begin urinating, and this stage is called a *foetus*.

Placental and uterine changes during the first trimester:

- *Uterine lining becomes thick with increased blood supply.* The uterus starts enlarging, the cervix becomes softer, and the implantation of the ovum is usually in the upper back portion of the uterus, where there is a formation of the *placenta* and the *umbilical cord*.
- By the end of 8 *weeks*, the uterus grows to a size of a tennis ball.
- By the end of 12 weeks, the size of the uterus is like a grapefruit, the fundus is just above the pubic bone, *amniotic fluids* fill the uterine cavity and is continually replaced. At this time, there is a complete exchange of nutrients and waste products through the placenta.

What are the common physical and emotional changes during the first trimester?

The following changes are observed in expectant mothers in this trimester:

- No menstruation
- Has fullness or aches in the pelvis
- May be nauseated and may vomit frequently
- Feel tired
- Has increased vaginal secretion
- May feel weak and faint.
- Urinate more frequently.

- ▶ Breasts are fuller, nipple may tingle and areola is darker.
- ▶ May lose or gain up to 2 to 2.5 kg of weight.
- ▶ Moods vary widely.
- ▶ There is always focus on body changes.
- ▶ Sexual relationship in both partners may change.
- ▶ May feel ambivalent towards pregnancy: joy and excitement *vs.* resentment and panic. Well-being of the baby remains a concern in both the partners.

Is sex during this period of pregnancy advisable?

Having sexual intercourse during pregnancy will not harm the foetus. One might continue sexual intercourse right up to the onset of labour. As the abdomen enlarges, a woman may find intercourse more comfortable in positions that put less or absolutely no pressure on abdomen like side-by-side or the female on the top. If you have complications like bleeding or pain in abdomen, refrain from sexual activity and even nipple stimulation is to be avoided in such cases as it can induce pre-term labour.

Doctors often advise to avoid intercourse from the 6th to the 12th week of pregnancy as it can cause miscarriage. *Sexual abstinence* is recommended during the last two months of pregnancy too. At this time, there is a risk of the essential amniotic fluid leakage during intercourse. However, the couple can and should engage in gentle love making, fondling and kissing. *Intercourse during the first three months and the last two months of pregnancy is not advisable.* During the 4th to 7th month of pregnancy, intercourse is allowed unless there are medical reasons. *Sexual act such as oral and anal sex should be strictly avoided throughout the pregnancy.*

My husband falls asleep after sex, why so?

Never mind. Unfortunately, men who fall asleep right after sex are merely giving in to biological forces. At orgasm, both he and you release the hormone *oxytocin*. It is the same chemical the body releases during breastfeeding, which make the baby sleepy. Men and women hold their breath while in the Process of lovemaking, in an effort to sustain the tension before a climax. *So, next time before reaching climax encourage your husband to take long, deep breathes.*

I am three months pregnant and feel ill sick all the time, and have terrible feeling of acidity. Suggest a solution.

Acidity, belching, and gas occur because of the growing baby. The enlarging uterus occupies more and more space in the abdomen and as a result, the stomach is pushed up. This leads to a reflux of the acid present in the stomach into the food pipe, leading to heartburn. The following precautions would help:

- ▶ Try taking small frequent meals so that the stomach is not very full at any given time.
- ▶ Avoid foods that cause acidity like *tea, coffee, colas, spicy and sour dishes, etc.*
- ▶ Stay upright after meals and take dinner at least two hours before bedtime.
- ▶ Take a glass of milk with honey to help heartburn.
- ▶ Consult your doctor to suggest antiacids to reduce acidity.

First Trimester of Pregnancy

I am pregnant since last two months. I want to know when should I visit my obstetrician for the first time during pregnancy and how often thereafter?

You should have visited your doctor as soon as you missed your periods, for there are certain conditions like:

- ▶ Thyroid disease
- ▶ Female hormone disorders that can also lead to missed periods

Pregnancy can be confirmed either by *urine test, internal examination or ultrasound.* Better visit your doctor.

If the pregnancy is confirmed, you should visit your doctor:

- ▶ Every month for the first seven months.
- ▶ Every two weeks between the 7th and the 8th month.
- ▶ Every week during the last month.

Chapter 3

Second Trimester of Pregnancy

Second Trimester

This second stage of pregnancy lasts until the end of the seventh month and in many times, the easiest stage of pregnancy as most women will start to regain some of their energy. *During this stage, your stomach will begin to expand and those around you will begin to notice that you are pregnant.* At this time, any feelings of *morning sickness* should dissipate, although some women may continue to experience it (usually to a lesser extent). *At this point, you may also feel your baby beginning to kick and move.* If you wish, you can find out whether you are having a girl or boy! However, this is not ethical on the part of the doctor.

Nutrition and Exercise

- ▶ 2500 calories per day
- ▶ Continue to maintain a well balanced diet with plenty of fibres.
- ▶ Continue to take prenatal vitamins, if prescribed.
- ▶ Continue to avoid the use of alcohol.
- ▶ Modify your exercise regimen if needed to protect the weight-bearing joints, back and abdominal muscles.
- ▶ Take care while lifting and carrying.

As you advance in this trimester of your pregnancy, you may notice that you feel more sensitive, emotional and anxious. Be rest assured, these feelings are very natural. It's common to begin worrying about what kind of mother you are going to be. Many times, the increased size and weight of your baby can cause increased pain (often in your back), making you feel more *uncomfortable and anxious.*

The following measures should be adopted:

- ▶ You may need small frequent feedings to prevent heartburn.
- ▶ Continue prenatal vitamins as prescribed.
- ▶ Adequate hydration and avoiding overheating are important to protect the baby and the mother.
- ▶ Further modify your exercise regimen as needed to protect your muscles and joints.

- ▶ Shortness of breath is common on exertion-You may need to reduce the intensity of your exercise regimen if you are becoming too winded.
- ▶ Stretch and tone to prepare for childbirth.

What are important signs and symptoms during the second trimester of pregnancy?

- ▶ Relief from nausea and vomiting.
- ▶ Desire to urinate frequently subsides.
- ▶ Movement of the growing baby in the womb is noticed by the 18th week in case of the first delivery, otherwise by the 16th week of pregnancy.
- ▶ Breasts start enlarging.
- ▶ Gradual increase of bulge in the abdomen.
- ▶ Skin around the nipples becomes dark.
- ▶ Clear watery secretion from the nipples becomes thick and yellowish, while squeezing by the 16th week.
- ▶ Small, pinkish and white streaks become visible on the lower abdomen.
- ▶ The skin of the upper thighs gets stretched by the 20th week.
- ▶ The appetite lost during the first trimester of pregnancy returns. There is nearly 20-25% increase in appetite.

What are the essential checks and tests during the second trimester of pregnancy?

- ▶ Have a regular check over the blood pressure. Consult a doctor in case the blood pressure starts rising, as it is harmful for the mother as well as the baby.
- ▶ Have a check over the growth of the baby in the womb during this period. After the 12th week, the womb lying deep in the pelvis starts rising out of the bony pelvis, which can be felt by placing a hand on the lower abdomen.
- ▶ Check the weight after the first trimester of pregnancy. The total weight gain during three trimesters of pregnancy should not be more than 10 to 12 kg. After the first trimester, there should be an increase in weight ranging from 0.7 to 1.4 kg. On completion of 20 weeks, the total increase in weight should be up to 4 kg. If the weight is more than the normal gain coupled with increase in blood pressure, consult a doctor immediately.
- ▶ Avoid excessive intake of heavy or spicy food.
- ▶ Ensure regular urine test for proteins as you may be suffering from *Pre-Eclamptic Toxaemia (PET)*, which is a common disorder in expectant mothers having High Blood Pressure.
- ▶ Around the 7th week of pregnancy, visit your doctor for an ultrasound. You can hear the baby's heartbeats around the 14th week of the pregnancy.
- ▶ A monthly urine test is a must to find out the traces of sugar indicating diabetes and proper functioning of the kidneys.
- ▶ Swelling of hands, ankles and legs should be examined by your doctor every time you go for check up, once a month.
- ▶ Have a haemoglobin test to detect the signs of anaemia.

- ▶ Even in case of a normal pregnancy, between 16th to 20th weeks of pregnancy, a routine ultrasound scan is advised to find out the growth of the child and position of the placenta. *In case the position of the placenta is near or on the cervical opening,* there are chances of severe bleeding and immediate attention of a doctor is required.
- ▶ Carry out the *Alpha Feto Protein* test during the *15th to the 18th week of pregnancy.* The Alpha Feto Protein is a substance produced by the baby, which passes into the mother's bloodstream. There are chances of congenital defect or there may be two babies in the womb, in case of abnormally high levels of this protein.
- ▶ *Amniocentosis* test is carried out between the 14th to 18th week of pregnancy to detect any abnormality in the baby. It is carried out only if the mother had delivered a malformed baby previously.
- ▶ During the second trimester of pregnancy, *tetanus toxoid injections* are administered twice at an interval of one month.

What to avoid during the second trimester of pregnancy?

- ▶ Do not take greasy and spicy foods to avoid chances of excessive weight gain.
- ▶ Drink 7 to 8 glasses of water in a day.
- ▶ Avoid constipation.
- ▶ Avoid excessive intake of sugar and salt.
- ▶ Avoid canned and processed foods. Take extra fruits and pulses.
- ▶ Avoid eating at unhygienic places.
- ▶ Sexual intercourse is not permissible in the second trimester of pregnancy in case of previous miscarriage or in case of vaginal bleeding. However, normal sex is permissible within the physical constraints imposed by the growing womb. A pregnant woman can, however, fulfill her husband's needs with love and tenderness, omitting intercourse. Doctors suggest intercourse in standing position or female lying over the male to avoid pressure on the belly.
- ▶ Avoid strenuous exercises in this trimester. Start with light exercises for 5 minutes and gradually increase the duration to not more than 10 minutes.
- ▶ Take complete bed rest if bleeding occurs.
- ▶ Do not exert to the point where you get tired. A walk in the open in the early morning is the best exercise during this period.
- ▶ Do not wear high-heeled shoes. Wear flat shoes as far as possible.
- ▶ Do not bend your waist, while picking up any object from the ground. Keep your back straight and bend at your knees and hips.
- ▶ Do not worry if there is burning sensation, while passing urine. Consult your doctor.
- ▶ In some cases, there is, burning sensation in the upper abdomen because the enlarged womb presses against the stomach pushing food contents up into the food pipe, resulting in pain and burning sensation in the upper abdomen and below the ribs. To prevent this, avoid taking spicy and fried foods.

- ▶ Take smaller quantities of food at short intervals instead of taking heavy meals at long intervals.
- ▶ Leakage of urine on light jerk is another common problem during the end of the second trimester of pregnancy due to a weak pelvic floor below the womb.
- ▶ Avoid lifting heavy weights and constipation. Empty your bladder frequently.
- ▶ A light pelvic exercise will help a lot. To exercise the pelvic region, lie on the floor with back and knees bent so that your feet lie flat touching the floor. Now tighten the muscles by pressing the hips and thighs drawing your vagina in as much as possible.
- ▶ Reddish, moist rashes may develop in the skin folds usually under the breasts and in the groin region, usually in the summer season during the last stage of pregnancy. The expectant mother should keep such area dry and clean.
- ▶ Avoid use of nylon underwears. Always use cotton undergarments.
- ▶ Painful contraction of muscles, usually in the calves, is another problem during the last of this trimester of pregnancy, generally due to *deficiency of calcium*. Take calcium tablets with the consultation of doctor. Massage the affected area and in case, the calves are affected, walk for sometime to regulate blood circulation.
- ▶ Heavy swelling of the feet, fingers and other parts on the body usually occur in late pregnancy and is called *Pre-Elcamptic Toxemia (PET)* – which is a combination of swelling on *ankles, fingers and vulva* (also known as the *oedema of vulva*) followed by puffiness of the face with increased blood pressure and presence of protein in urine.
- ▶ The risk of PET is more common among obese women and females getting married in teenage. Women with family history of high blood pressure are prone to this risk and should consult a doctor immediately. A delayed treatment may cause a *risk of fits and birth of a retarded child.*
- ▶ An expectant mother in the habit of smoking and drinking causes severe damage to the baby in the womb. Intra-uterine growth retardation is a condition where the growth of the baby in the womb is severely impaired due to anaemia and malnourishment. To ensure a healthy baby, it is important to completely part with smoking and taking alcohol.
- ▶ Remember, smoking is the root cause of certain diseases like *high blood pressure, chronic kidney diseases, heart ailments and several infections harmful to the mother as well as for the child's health and growth. Excessive smoking affects the production of breast milk and alcohol taken by the mother passed into the baby causing severe side effects.*
- ▶ The gums start bleeding and become inflamed during the last trimester of pregnancy. Brush your teeth thoroughly after taking meals and massage the gums gently.
- ▶ There is a complaint of leakage of urine, while walking briskly, laughing or sneezing by the expecting mothers during this and the last trimester of pregnancy due to loss of strength of the muscles of the pelvic floor, which support the *intestines, urinary bladder and the womb.*

- *Expectant mothers develop the problem of piles due to constant pressure of the baby on the blood vessels around the anal region.* This also results in soreness, itching pain and bleeding, while passing stool. Avoid constipation and standing for a long time. Consult a doctor to prescribe an ointment to reduce pain and itching.
- The expectant mothers feel uneasy and cannot sleep properly in the night usually during the *3rd trimester of pregnancy.* Reading or a warm bath before going to sleep helps a lot. Lie on your side with a pillow under the head.
- Constipation is another problem common during the second and the third trimester because the bowel movement slows down under the influence of *progesterone hormone.* As such, the stools become hard and infrequent. *Take plenty of fluids besides regular exercise. Avoid laxatives, and consult a doctor.*
- *Problem of excess sweating arises during the last trimester of pregnancy,* generally attributed to *hormonal changes.* Wear loose clothes, especially during night and take plenty of water.
- Many times, there is a thick curd-like discharge with severe itching in the vaginal region. A slight increase in the clear or whitish vaginal secretion is normal. The hormonal changes during the last trimester of pregnancy make one more prone to vaginal thrush with a thick discharge and itching, which make urination painful. Avoid use of soap and nylon undergarments and keep the area around the vagina dry and clean.
- The risk of complications during delivery is more pronounced in women suffering from anaemia. The Red Blood Cells (RBCs) contain a substance called *haemoglobin, which carries oxygen. The normal level of haemoglobin is 11 to 14 gm.* In case, its level falls to below 10 gm, one is considered anaemic. An anaemic expectant mother may have a smaller than the normal child or a premature baby. The risk of pregnancies also increases during delivery in the anaemic women.

What are the common developments during the second stage of pregnancy?

Some of common developments are listed below. In case, you find any change in the developments, seek the advice of your doctor or gynaecologist :

Foetal growth: Till the 16th week, the foetal is 6 inches long with strong heart beats, active muscles, thin and transparent skin, downy hair covering the body, formation of fingernails and toenails. By the end of the 20th week, the foetal length reaches 10 to 12 inches, and there is the presence of hair, eyelashes and eyebrows. By the end of the 24th week, the foetal length reaches to 11 to 14 inches, the skin gets wrinkled and the meconium starts collecting in the bowel.

Placental and uterine changes: Till the end of the 16th week, the uterus is placed 3 inches above the pubic bone and the placenta performs *nutritional, respiratory, excretory* and most of the endocrine functions. The amniotic fluid increases in amount. By the end of the 20th week, the uterus is placed at the level of navel and the size of placenta covers half of the inner surface of the uterus. By the end of 24 weeks, the uterus reaches above the level of the navel.

Second Trimester of Pregnancy

These are the following common physical and emotional changes in a pregnant woman:

- ▶ Foetal movement is noticeable.
- ▶ There is no nausea during this stage.
- ▶ Women usually become constipated.
- ▶ Have food cravings.
- ▶ Sometimes develop *vaginitis* (thick vaginal discharge)
- ▶ There is a usual problem of nasal congestion.
- ▶ Have leg cramps frequently.
- ▶ Change in voice.
- ▶ Painful groin from the round ligament contractions.
- ▶ Weight gain.
- ▶ Pregnancy becomes more enjoyable.
- ▶ Sexual desires may increase.

Sometimes, I have leakage of milk from the breast nipples. What to do?

Breasts are felt hard, sore and soaked because of milk secretion from the breasts in the early or mid pregnancy often in the morning. Consult a gynaecologist who will teach you how to take care of the breasts during pregnancy. Give a firm support to the breasts using a good quality and correct-sized brassier to match the cups, which should be loose and supportive, but not tight. Light exercise for the breast keeps the breast disorders at bay.

What is 4-D ultrasound?

A 4-D *Ultrasound* is the latest addition in the armamentarium of an obstetrician. *A 3-D Ultrasound gives a 3-D or three dimensional view of the baby* in the womb. An ultrasound

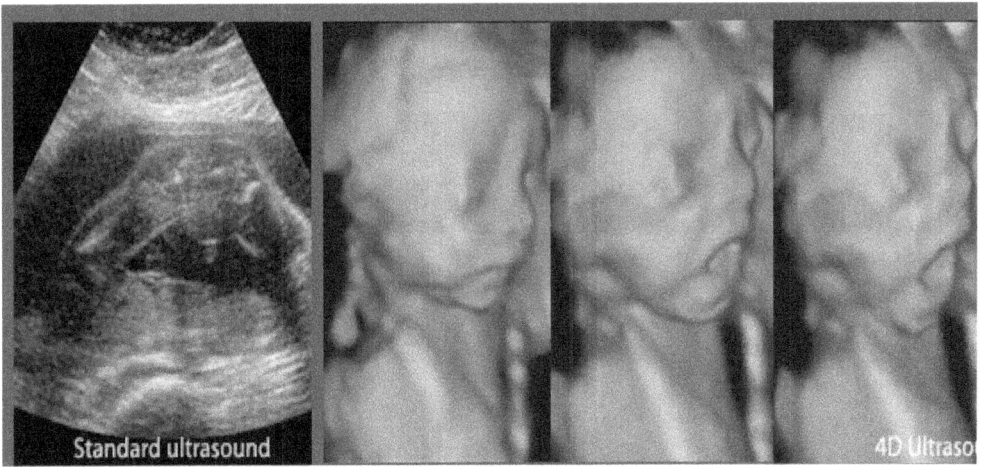

4 - D Ultrasound

gives a 2D dimensional view, which makes the diagnosis of the malformations and the surface of the body of the baby and internal malformations can be visualised clearly. A *3-D Ultrasound* is like a still photograph, whereas, a 3D Ultrasound is like taking a video film of the foetus malformation and the pregnancy, especially in case the mother is over the age of 35 years and has delivered a malformed baby in the past.

Queries usually pregnant women ask during the second stage of pregnancy:

I am having stretch marks on my abdomen and stomach. What should I do?

Stretch marks on the abdomen and stomach are common in women generally during pregnancy and after the delivery of the child. *Striae gravidarum* or *stretch marks* appear on the lower abdomen in 50 to 90 percent of all pregnant women usually in the later half of pregnancy. These may also appear on the *thighs, hips, buttocks, breasts and the upper arms of women,* which appear as pinkish lines on fair complexioned women and lighter than the normal skin in dark complexioned women. The market is flushed with creams and ointments to cure these stretch marks. The stretch marks depend upon the *family history, weight gain and nutritional status.* These marks are called the *Striac Marks.*

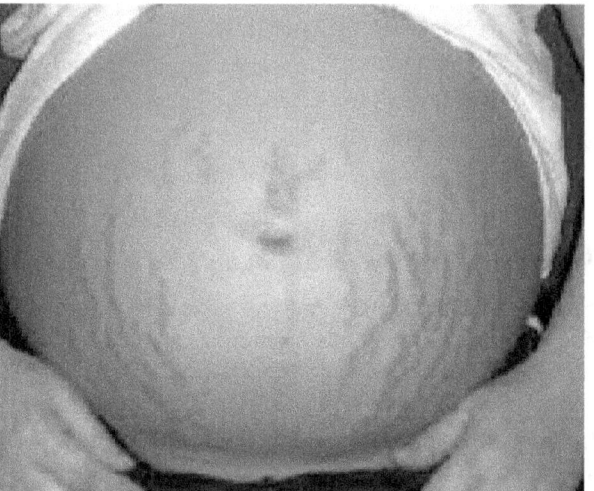

Striac Marks

What to do in case of cramps and pains in the abdomen?

Between 30 to 50%, women suffer *cramps pain* during this period. *Persistent night cramps* are often caused by *poor circulation*. The cramp felt in the abdomen are difficult to cope but doesn't show that there is any abnormality in the genitals of the woman. There are several natural remedies to cure this painful disorder as below:

- ▶ Add seven drops of essential oil of aromatic spicy herb cloves to a teaspoon of sunflower oil and massage the muscles of the affected area.
- ▶ Tincture of myrrh rubbed directly into the affected muscle, gives a quick relief.
- ▶ Mix two drops of each of the essential oils of lemon, pine and juniper, and shake with 1 tablespoon of sunflower oil and massage.

Is morning sex permissible during the second stage of pregnancy?

Early morning is the best time to have sex due to the following reasons, but avoid heavy jerks and weight on the belly during this period:

- ▶ The testosterone level in the male partner is higher in the early morning hours.
- ▶ Men and women have higher levels of growth of the hormones due to increased energy after the restful night.
- ▶ Often a man awakes with a full bladder, which compresses the venous blood return and prevents blood escaping from the penis. As a result, the male partner experiences spontaneous erections in the morning.

Second Trimester of Pregnancy

▶ Sex during the night when the blood flow to the digestive system is predominant lacks pleasure. Good sex act requires good blood flow towards the sex organs and is achieved better in the morning with empty stomach.

Why ovary cancer is frequent among women?

Ovary cancer is common in women due to frequent childbirth resulting in wear and tear of the cervical tissue and natural genital secretions. The following symptoms are observed when the patient suffers from cervical cancer:

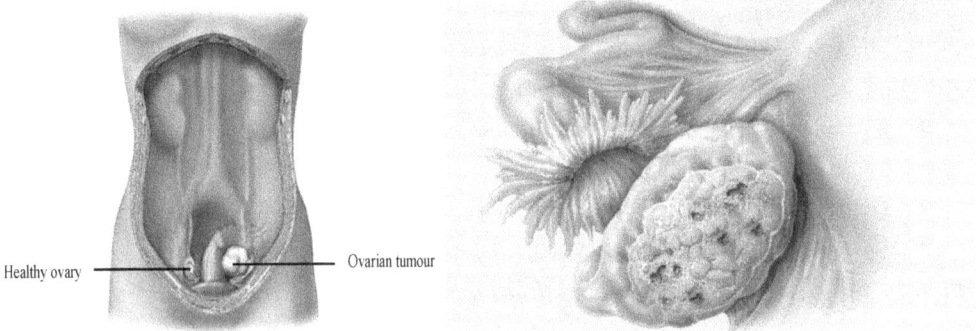

Ovary Cancer

▶ Abnormal blood stained vaginal discharge.
▶ Intermittent prolonged menstrual bleeding.
▶ Intercourse bringing on bleeding.
▶ Foul smelling and vaginal secretion.
▶ Pain in the lower abdomen.
▶ Constant backache.
▶ Wear and tear of cervical tissues.

To treat cancer of the cervix, measures such as surgical removal of the affected part and destroying cancerous cells by radium or cobalt are adopted. If not treated at the initial stage, the cancerous cells may spread to the liver and the brain.

Why Pre-elcamptic Toxemia is common in pregnant women?

Pre-elcamptic Toxemia (PET) is a combination of Oedema (e.g. swelling on the ankles and fingers followed by puffiness of the face, with increased blood pressure and presence of protein in the urine). Obese women and teenage pregnant are usually seen suffering from this disorder. Women with family history of High Blood Pressure are proned to this risk. In case, it is not timely treated, there may be serious conditions of fits and the birth of a retarded child due to infra-uterine growth affecting the growth

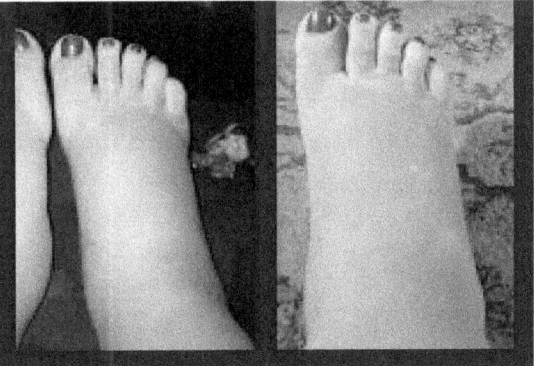

Toxemia

of the infant in the womb. The disease is more common in anaemic and malnourished women. *For a healthy growth of unborn baby*, it *is important to part with smoking and alcohol*. Certain conditions like high blood pressure, chronic kidney diseases, heart ailments and some infections also affect the baby's growth.

What to do in case of heartburn?

Heartburn – A feeling of fullness is a common complaint in the late second stage or the third stage of pregnancy caused by combination of the hormonal effects that relax the muscular opening, cause the stomach to empty more slowly and increase pressure from the growing uterus. Fatty foods, foods that produce gas and large meals may contribute to such condition.

The following treatment is recommended:

- ▶ Avoid fatty foods and foods that produce gas.
- ▶ Eat several small meals and eat slowly.
- ▶ Do not eat just before bedtime.
- ▶ Use antacid or other drugs to control heartburn.

What to do in case of frequent constipation?

During pregnancy, the movement of food through the intestines is slowed due to pressure from the growing uterus on the large intestine which magnifies the problem. Drink plenty of fluids. Eat foods with high fibre content, such as raw or dried fruits, vegetables, whole grains and pruned juice. Preventing constipation also alleviates the discomfort of haemorrhoids during pregnancy.

What to do in case of sudden pain in the back that moves towards the right shoulder?

It is common during pregnancy and generally starts durning night when pain suddenly begins from the back and radiates to the right shoulder. To get relief, press the stomach. Sometimes, this pain may be due to accumulation of acidity in the gall bladder. *In case the pain is due to the liver or the kidney, a complete bed rest is advised.*

I have pain in the stomach and the lower belly frequently. What should I do?

Mild stomach or liver pain during pregnancy is not a matter of worry and is usually caused due to increased weight of the embryo and mother's nerves getting strained. Massage the stomach lightly with *ghee* or *butter* to get relief. Constant pain in the lower belly should be brought to the notice of the doctor. A weak pregnant woman may have several abdominal discomforts during early pregnancy due to infection in the pelvic organs or the urinary tract.

A drop or two of blood oozes from the uterus, what to do?

This problem usually develops during the 4th and the 5th month from the date of conception and sometimes, may lead to *miscarriage*. There is a small membrane in the uterus filled with *amniotic fluid* in which the *foetus* develops. In some cases, the membrane gets swollen and the *placenta orifice* gets closed due to inflammation. This leads to the placenta puffing up and blood mixed with water accumulates in the region. Take your doctor's advice.

Second Trimester of Pregnancy

Have severe itching, pain in the vagina after intercourse. Can you suggest a remedy?

It could be either due to semen remaining in the vagina after intercourse or abrasion in the vaginal tract caused due to friction. It is suggested to avoid sex during this stage. If possible, avoid intercourse during the entire period of pregnancy, as it may harm the child. The itching and the pain may spread to the anus also. Better take suggestions of a doctor.

What is the cause of a sudden increase in weight and swelling of the body?

Signs like sudden increase in weight, swelling of the body, rise in blood pressure, appearance of albumin in urine, severe breathing trouble, constant thumping of the heart and abrupt bleeding are the warning signs that something is wrong with the pregnancy. Go for immediate medical advice. The pregnant woman must have a periodical check on *weight, blood pressure* and urine. A woman should not put more than 10 kg of weight during the entire period of pregnancy. There is often an increase of weight from the 3rd month onwards. Take a low salt but high protein diet.

What is the cause of weakness, insomnia and exhaustion during the second stage of pregnancy?

Feeling too weak and exhausted, loss of sleep (insomnia), especially during night, a constant tension, loss of appetite and constant fever are common disorders among women during pregnancy because of a growing embryo.

The following home remedies can alleviate the problems:

- Mix two parts each of pumpkin oil and poppy seed oil to a part of camphor and massage the head daily in the morning and evening.
- Massage the head with *Brahmi* or *Narayan* or *Mahanarayan oil*.
- Take *Sarpagandatvaka Churan* mixed in hot milk during night for a sound sleep.

I am suffering from piles? What should I do during pregnancy?

Piles generally develops due to *faulty food habits, irregular bowel routine, taking spicy foods* and *as a result of constipation*, which irritate the stomach and the intestines. In pregnant woman, piles usually develop due to *abdominal pressure*. It is better to maintain proper *bowel habits*. Early cases of piles are treated with local anaesthetics and ointments. In severe cases, pile masses are pricked with syringes to shrink them. In some cases, piles develop a couple of months after the delivery.

What are the common skin diseases associated with pregnancy?

In a study conducted on pregnant women, most of them were found to have some lesions involving the skin.

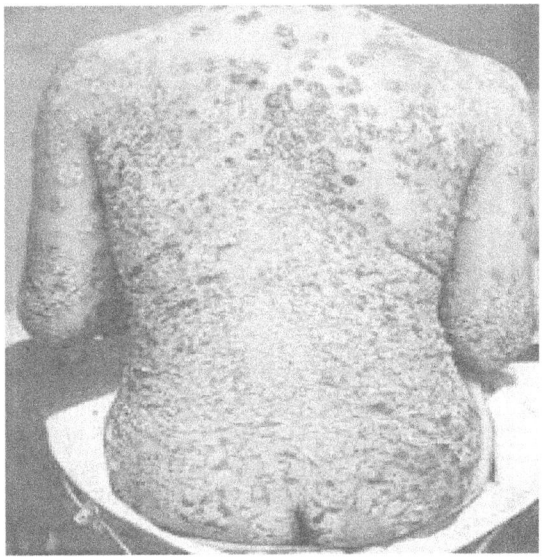

Skin Diseases

The following are the more important physiological changes, which affect the skin of the pregnant woman as described in the following:

Pigmentation:

This occurs in about 75% pregnant women by the end of the second and last trimester. The commonest and most characteristic site for pigmentation is the face and the forehead, where it is known as 'Chloasma'. The cause of pregnancy pigmentation is due to increased production of *progesterone*, which directly affects the *melanocytes*.

Other pigmentary changes occurring during this stage of pregnancy are the following:

Pigmentation

- ▶ Hyperpigmentation of pigmented areas, especially of the vulva and labia, areola, nipples and umbilicus.
- ▶ Pigmentation of *linea alba* usually developing in the 4th month of pregnancy.
- ▶ The *linea nigra fusca* – pigmentation running from the mons to the umbilicus.
- ▶ Pigment marks on and around the areola on the breasts.

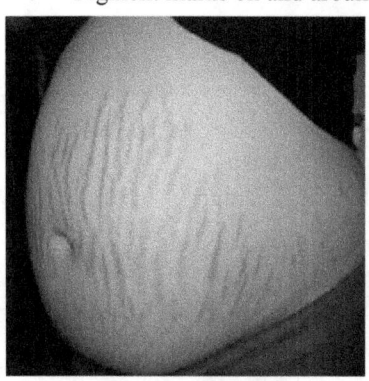

Striae Gravidarum

Striae Gravidarum

Almost 75% women usually suffer from this disorder by the 6th month of pregnancy, which appear as thin, clear-cut lines of atrophy in parallel or in curves on the abdomen, breasts, flanks, lumbar and sacral regions, hips and inner side of the thighs. The lines become less conspicuous with the passage of time after delivery.

Erythema of palms

Present as *mottled erythema* and distributed on the entire surface of the palm, which increases with the advance of pregnancy, Erythema is found to be present in 60% of the fair complexioned women and 40% of the dark complexioned women. It fades in 90% of the cases within 6 to 8 weeks after delivery.

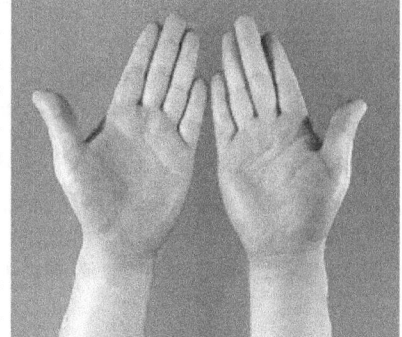

Erythema of Palms

Multiple spider naevi

Bright red lesions usually appear during the third and the fifth month of pregnancy and slowly increases in size mainly on the face, neck, upper arms and the chest. About 75% of the lesions disappear completely within two months of delivery and sometimes remain incurable even for years. The cause of *spider naevi* is due to hormonal reasons.

Molluscum fibroma gravidarum

These contagious lesions is also caused by virus due to epidermal hyperplasia and consist of a core of connective tissues without any elastic tissue covered by the epidermis. They appear during the second half of pregnancy on the front, sides, nape of the neck, in the axillae, on the breast and the upper chest.

Skin diseases during the second stage of pregnancy

These include *pruigo gestationis, herpes gestationis, impeligo herpetiformus, papular dermatitis* of pregnancy, *lesions of prurigo, macules, papules, excoriations, lichenification, urticarial eruptions, eczematous eruptions, erythemas* and *scabies*. Most of these eruptions develop in the late second stage or the third stage of pregnancy. Irritation and rashes disappear in 7 to 14 days with proper medication prescribed by the doctor.

Herpes gestationis

Lesions develop in the first trimester of pregnancy or during the successive pregnancies due to hormonal changes in which lesions develop during the second trimester of pregnancy and usually itching and burning between the age of 30 to 35 years. It starts clearing within 30 days after the pregnancy. The patches may become pustular or haemorrhagia and the rashes spread. Eventually, the whole body may be involved. The lesions regress and heal leaving behind pigmentation.

Papular dermatitis of pregnancy

The symptoms include intense itching lesions widely scattered over the trunk, arms, legs, face and scalp throughout the pregnancy. The condition is associated with a high foetal mortality. Consult a doctor for treatment.

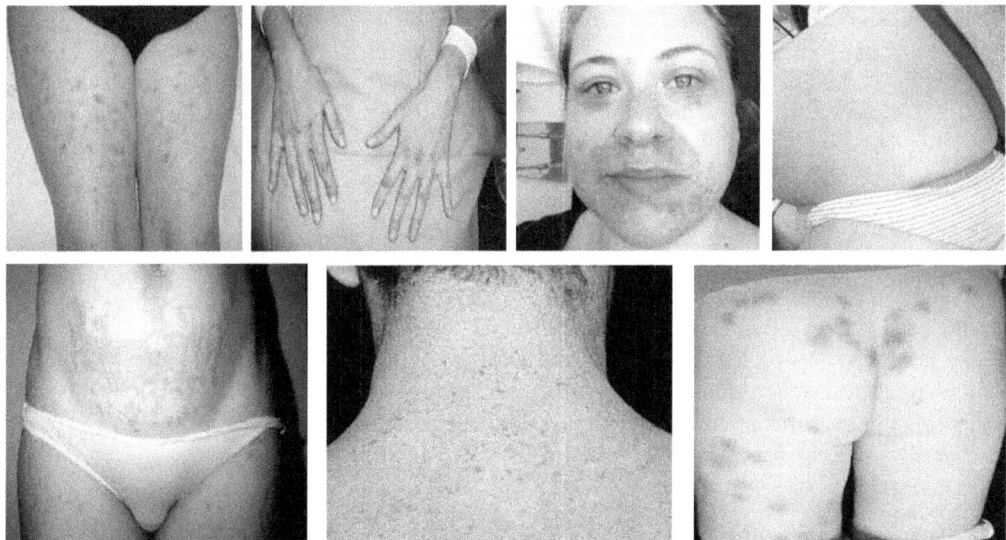

Papular Dermatitis

Intertrigo (Intertriginous Dermatitis)

An highly inflammatory reaction of the epidermis, which occur in the region of the body folds or area on the skin surfaces in close contact. The causes of this disease are friction, sweating and heat, which lead inevitably to reddening, scales, soreness and irritation and maceration of the epidermis of skin followed by infection, erosions and fissures with skin organism, fungi or yeasts, especially *candida albicans*. The treatment includes soothing the inflammation, keeping affected skin clean with soap and water, sitz baths or foot baths of potassium permanganate solution for minimum 10 minutes or wet dressings of potassium permanganate, application of steroid lotions or creams and fungicidal ointment, control over obesity, diabetes and glycosuria.

Psoriasis

This skin disease is common during pregnancy on limbs and trunks usually due *to friction, moisture* and *overweight*. To cure psoriasis, warm or potassium permanganate baths are suggested followed by application of steroid lotion or cream. If untreated, it leads to the risk of *irritant dermatitis* or *sensitisation*.

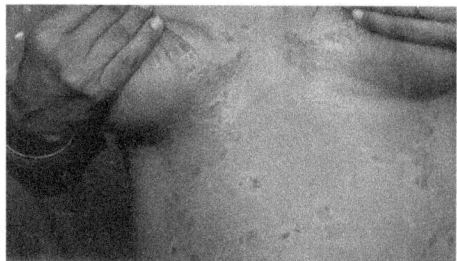
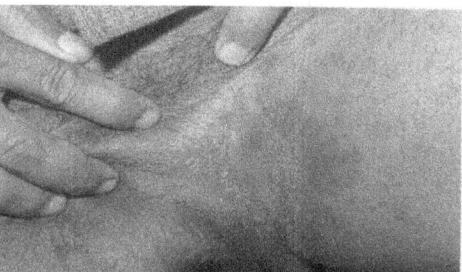

Psoriasis

Eczema and Scabies

The areola and the nipple are common sites for eczema on the body of a pregnant woman having eczematous lesions on the breasts, wrists, anterior and posterior axillary folds usually appearing on skin creases.

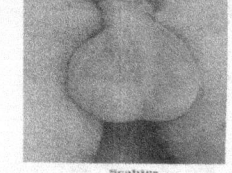

Condyloma Acuminate

When warts start oozing, growing rapidly in pregnant women with offensive odour generally affecting external genitalia, pre-anal region and perineum. This contagious virus disease of the skin spreads in the moist, medium and becomes very proliferative in the presence of vaginal discharges and venereal diseases or other infections. To have a curb over this disease, scrupulous cleanliness of the affected area is essential and all vaginal discharges should be investigated.

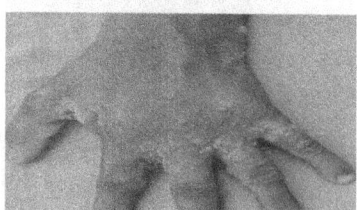

Papular Dermatitis

Pityriasis Versicolour

It is a fungus skin disease in pregnant women generally characterised by round *macules*. The colour of lesions varies from light to deep brown giving an appearance of hyperpigmentation accompanied by scales. It is difficult to cure this disease during pregnancy. To treat the disorder, wash the affected areas thoroughly having daily hot bath, application of a 10% solution of sodium thiosulphate with a brush or applying ointment containing sulphur and salicylic acid.

Candidiasis

Nearly 25% of the pregnant women suffer from this disease in the vaginal area and attribute to the increased amount of glycogen present in the vaginal cells. Candidiasis is classified into three groups: *cutaneous and mucosal thrush, secondary eruptions due to yeasts* and *monilial granulomata.*

Monilial vulvo-vaginitis

There is chronic vaginal discharge in this disorder. Heavy leucorrhoea discharge during pregnancy causes fungus. The symptoms include *pruritus vulvae* and *soreness of introitus, odema, excoriation* and *lichenification of the labia* and *perineal region, congestion* and *reddening of the vaginal mucosa, white patches* accompanied by *fungus* on the *labia and vaginal wall.* Consult a doctor immediately. The remedial measures include daily sitz bath in the solution of potassium permanganate solution, insertion of nystatin pessaries into the vagina at night and in the morning for 2 to 4 weeks in consultation with your doctor.

Trichomoniasis

Infection is the common cause of vaginal discharge and vulvo-vaginitis occurring in pregnant as well as non-pregnant women, which may be transmitted to the male during intercourse giving rise to *urethritis, palano-posthitis* and *chronic prostatitis*. The main symptoms of this disease are *pruritus vulvae, odema* and *redness of the vulva* with frothy vaginal discharge. To clear infection, oral therapy and insertion of pessaries have shown 80% curative effects. If repeated relapses occur in married women, it is advisable to treat the husband also.

Pruritus in pregnancy

Common skin disorders during the second and third trimester of pregnancy, which interferes with sleep and exhausts the patient mentally and physically, localised to the vulva or the peri-anal regions often associated with pain, itching, striae gravidarum, urticaria, scabies and varicosities of the vulva. The causes of generalised pruritus include dermatoses related to pregnancy, metabolic disorders (such as diabetes, jaundice and uraemia), leukemia (blood dyscrasiois), skin diseases (eczema, dermatitis, scabies, herpetiformis and herpes gestationis), malignant abdominal and pelvic diseases, lack of personal cleanliness, bacterial infection of inguinal folds, excessive vaginal discharge, pediculosis pubis, use of contraceptive pessaries and creams, contact dermatitis due to sanitary pads and nylon underclothes. To treat the disorder, remove the cause, if possible. Apply *corticosteroid creams* or lotions in consultation with the doctor. *Tepid baths* are helpful to treat this disorder.

Chapter 4

Third Trimester of Pregnancy

What essential precautions a pregnant woman should take during the third week of pregnancy?

The period from 29th to 40th week of pregnancy is the last stage of pregnancy, and this needs a lot of care. As the arrival of a new baby draws nearer, expecting mothers are filled with excitement to see the new arrival as well as the fear of the delivery of a child increases. The expectant mother should visit a doctor once a week in case of any complication or once in a fortnight in case of normal condition. During the final month of pregnancy, between the 37th to the 40th weeks, the following medical check up and precautions are essential:

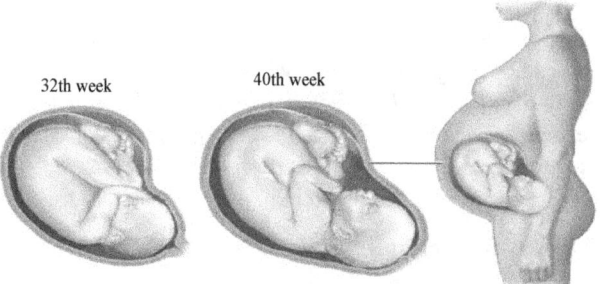

Third Timester of Pregnany

- ▶ There must be three or more movements of the baby in an hour during the last week of pregnancy. In case the movements are less, consult your doctor.
- ▶ Get your blood pressure checked once a week and urine once a fortnight.
- ▶ Check any swelling on the face and feet and in case of swelling, inform your doctor.
- ▶ Consult your doctor for finding the position of the baby in the womb, size and growth, heartbeats of the baby by an abdominal examination, which help during the process of delivery.
- ▶ In case you find any abnormality in the breast nipples, consult your doctor. A nipple exercise will be beneficial to treat disorders.
- ▶ Avoid sex during this period as it becomes cumbersome and physically difficult because of a bulging abdomen. Sex should strictly be avoided if there is a history of bleeding during pregnancy or there is a risk of premature birth of a baby. However, there is no harm doing intercourse carefully after consulting your doctor lying in such a position that there is no pressure at all on the abdomen.
- ▶ Take 8 to 10 hours of sleep during the night and minimum of 3 to 4 hours rest during the day.
- ▶ Continue very light exercises during this trimester, which are important for good health.

Make sure the exercises are done to the extent where you do not get tired. Consult your doctor before starting the exercises.

- You may feel breathlessness and discomfort during the last two months of pregnancy usually due to the growing womb, which pushes the other abdominal organs upward. In such condition, rest as much as possible. Use an extra pillow to prop yourself up, while lying down.
- In case you feel dizzy during the last four weeks of pregnancy, generally due to low blood pressure, take complete rest.
- Avoid standing for a long period.
- There is often a feeling of *frequent urination during night in the last 8 to 10 weeks of pregnancy, generally due to the womb pressing down on the bladder.*
- In some cases, there is a burning sensation in the upper abdomen during the last phase of pregnancy because the enlarged womb presses against the stomach, thus pushing the food contents up into the food pipe resulting in pain and burning sensation in the upper abdomen and below the ribs. To prevent this, avoid taking spicy and fried foods. Take smaller quantities of food at short intervals instead of taking heavy meals at long intervals.
- Leakage of urine on light jerk is another common problem during the last trimester of pregnancy due to weak pelvic floor below the womb. Avoid lifting heavy weights and constipation. Empty your bladder frequently. A light pelvic exercise will help a lot. To exercise the pelvic region, lie on the floor with back and knees bent so that your feet lie flat touching the floor. Now tighten the muscles by pressing the hips and thighs drawing your vagina in as much as possible.
- Reddish, moist rashes may develop in the skin folds usually under the breasts and in the groin region during the last stage of pregnancy, generally in summer. The expectant mother should keep such area dry and clean. Avoid use of nylon underwear. Always use cotton undergarments.
- Painful contraction of muscles, usually in the calves, is another problem during the last trimester of pregnancy, generally due to deficiency of calcium. *Take calcium tablets with the consultation of doctor. Massage the affected area and in case the calves are affected, walk for sometime to regulate blood circulation.*
- Heavy swelling of the feet, fingers and other parts on the body usually occur in late pregnancy and is called *Pre-Elcamptic Toxemia* (PET) – which is a combination of swelling on the ankles, fingers and vulva (also known as oedema of vulva) followed by puffiness of the face with increased blood pressure and presence of protein in urine. The risk of PET is more common among obese women and females getting married in teenage. Women with family history of high blood pressure are prone to this risk and consult a doctor immediately. A delayed treatment may cause a risk of fits and birth of a retarded child.
- An expectant mother in the habit of smoking and drinking cause severe damage to the baby in the womb. Intra-uterine growth retardation is a condition where the growth of the baby in the womb is severely impaired due to *anaemia and malnourishment.* To ensure a healthy baby, it is important to completely part with smoking and taking alcohol. Smoking is the root cause of certain diseases like high blood pressure, chronic kidney diseases, heart ailments and several infections harmful for the mother as well as

- for the child's health and growth. Excessive smoking affects the production of breast milk and alcohol taken by the mother passed into the baby causes severe side effects.
- ▶ The gums start bleeding and become inflamed during the last trimester of pregnancy. Brush your teeth thoroughly after taking meal and massage your gums gently.
- ▶ There is a complaint of leakage of urine, while walking briskly, laughing or sneezing by the expecting mothers during the last trimester of pregnancy which is mainly due to loss of strength of the muscles of the pelvic floor, which support the intestines, urinary bladder and the womb. Here is an exercise to treat this disorder. Lie on the floor with back and knees bent keeping the feet flat on the ground. Tighten the muscles, squeezing as if trying to stop the urine. Draw your vagina in, pause for a while and then relax. Repeat for 10 to 15 times.
- ▶ *Expectant mothers develop the problem of piles in the last trimester of pregnancy* due to constant pressure of the baby on blood vessels around the anal region. This also results in soreness, itching pain and bleeding, while passing stool. Avoid constipation and standing for a long time. Consult a doctor to prescribe an ointment to reduce the pain and itching.
- ▶ The expectant mothers feel uneasy and cannot sleep properly in the night usually during the third trimester of pregnancy. Reading or a warm bath before going to sleep helps a lot. Lie on your side with a pillow under the head.
- ▶ Constipation is another problem common during the third trimester because the bowel movement slows down under the influence of progesterone hormone. As such the stools become hard and infrequent. Take plenty of fluids besides regular exercise. *Avoid laxatives*. Consult a doctor.
- ▶ Problem of excess sweating arises during the last trimester of pregnancy generally attributed to hormonal changes. Wear loose clothes, especially during night and take plenty of water.
- ▶ Many times, there is thick curd-like discharge with severe itching in the vaginal region. A slight increase in the clear or whitish vaginal secretion is normal. The hormonal changes during the last trimester of pregnancy makes one more proned to vaginal thrush with a thick discharge and itching, which make urination painful. Avoid the use of soap and nylon undergarments and keep the area around the vagina dry.
- ▶ The risk of complications during delivery is more pronounced in women suffering from anaemia. The Red Blood Cells contain a substance called *haemoglobin*, which carries *oxygen*. The normal level of haemoglobin is 11 to 14 gm. In case, its level falls to below 10 gm, one is considered anaemic. An anaemic expectant mother may have a smaller than the normal child or a premature baby. The risk of pregnancies also increases during delivery in anaemic women.
- ▶ Multistage pregnancy can easily be diagnosed by the size of the womb or during *USG scanning*. In case of a multiple pregnancy, consult your doctor more frequently and take complete rest between the 30th to 37th week to avoid premature delivery. There may be a possibility of a *caesarian section* in case of a *multiple pregnancy*. In case of caesarian section, the delivery of a baby is made through an incision in the uterus rather than the baby's exit through cervix and vagina where incision is done in the low lying transverse region in the lower abdomen where the baby is hidden under the pubic hair.

Third Trimester of Pregnancy

Give some essential information about the unborn baby in the womb in the third phase of pregnancy?

Foetal growth: Reaches to about 20 inches. Fingernails protrude beyond fingers. The head is large as compared to the body. The arms and legs are in flexed position, and the lungs become mature.

Placental and uterine changes: The uterus is back to height at the 34th week. The placenta with one inch thickness has 6 to 8 inches diameter. The umbilical cord has a length of approximately 20 to 22 inches (sometimes ranges between 12 to 39 inches also) and has twisted or spiral appearance.

Common physical and emotional changes: Contractions, bloody show, progressive effacement and dilation, backache, ruptured membranes and loose bowel movements are some of the signs of labour.

What are the warning signs during the second phase of pregnancy?

Inform in case of any of the following warning signs to your doctor:

Warning Signs	*Possible Problems*
Excessive vaginal bleeding:	Miscarriage, Placenta previa, bruptio placenta, Premature labour.
Abdominal pain	Ectopic pregnancy, Abruptio placenta, Early labour contractions.
Leaking or gushing of fluid from the vagina:	Rupture of the membranes.
Puffiness or swelling of hands, feet, or face:	Pre-eclampsia (toxemia).
Severe, persistent headache:	Pre-eclampsia (toxemia).
Vision disturbance, blind spots and flashes:	Pre-eclampsia (toxemia).
Dizziness, light headedness, hypotension:	Pre-eclampsia or supine hypotension.
Pain or burning on urination:	Urinary tract infection, Sexually transmitted disease.
Irritating vaginal discharge, sores, itching:	Vaginal infection and STD.
Fever (oral temperature):	Infection.
Persistent nausea or vomiting:	Hyperemesis gravidarum and infection.
Noticeable reduction in foetal activity:	Foetal distress.

Is perineum massage useful for painless delivery?

Yes, it is used to soften the tissue around the vagina, relax the pelvic floor muscles and increase the elasticity of the perineum by taking advantage of the hormonal changes that loosen the connective tissue in late pregnancy, when there is pressure before and during birth. A regular perineum massage at least 6 to 8 weeks before the due date of delivery helps avoiding an episiotomy (vaginal cut at the time of delivery), or any tear during childbirth. Remember, if you have vaginitis, herpes or other vaginal problems, be sure to get checked before starting perineum massage, as it could worsen the condition. You can do self-massage or seek the help of your partner. Wash your hands before massaging. Be sure that your fingernails are short. If the skin of the hands is rough, wear disposable rubber gloves. Sit in a comfortable semi-sitting position squatting against a wall or sitting on the toilet seat.

The following procedure should be adopted, while doing perineum massage:

- ▶ Lubricate your fingers with oil or water-soluble jelly. Wheat-germ oil is recommended, as it contains high Vitamin E content. Do not use mineral oil or petroleum jelly. Wash your hands every time before dipping into the lubricant.
- ▶ Rub enough oil or jelly into the perineum to allow your fingers move smoothly over the tissue and lower the vaginal wall.
- ▶ You may use your thumb during self-massage or your partner can use his index finger. Put the fingers or thumb well inside the vagina up to the second knuckle, move them upward along the sides of the vagina in a *rhythmic U or sling-type movement* to help stretching the vaginal tissues, and muscles around the vagina and smoothen the skin of the perineum by rubbing between the thumb and the forefinger.
- ▶ Concentrate on relaxing your muscles as you apply pressure comfortably.
- ▶ Massage for about five minutes.

How to strengthen the pelvic floor muscles?

The pelvic floor or the perineum muscles act as a support to your abdominal and pelvic organs, which usually sag during pregnancy due to the increased weight of your uterus and the relaxing

 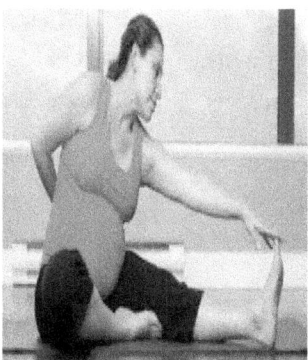 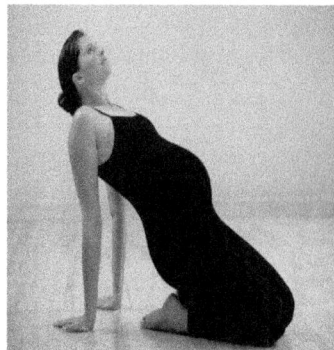

Third Trimester of Pregnancy

effect of the hormones produced by your body. A regular exercise of the pelvic floor muscles (which forms a figure 8, circling around the urethra, vagina and anus) maintain the tone, improve circulation and reduce the heavy, throbbing feeling that you might experience during this period of pregnancy. A regular exercise of the pelvic floor is important during pregnancy as well as throughout your lifetime, which also increase the sexual enjoyment for you and your partner. Problems, such as leakage of urine and relaxation of the rectal wall can also be prevented or reduced if the muscle of the pelvic floor is maintained. To check the strength of your pelvic floor muscles, try to stop the flow of urine in the midstream. You may also check by inserting two fingers in the vagina and tightening your pelvic floor muscles around them. At the time of intercourse, check by tightening your pelvic floor muscles around your partner's genital organ (penis).

The following exercise movements are suggested:

- **Pelvic floor contraction (Perineal squeeze or Kegal exercise):** This maintains the tone of the pelvic floor muscles, and improves circulation to the perineum. Contract or tighten the pelvic muscles as if you would stop the flow of urine. Hold tightly for 2-3 seconds, release tension, relax and lower the pelvic floor. Repeat several times.
- **Squatting:** This exercise increases the mobility of the pelvic joints, the stretch and the muscles and ligaments of the inner thighs and calves. It eases delivery of the child. Slowly squat with your weight on your whole foot, not just your toes as if you are sitting for toilet. Stay down for 30 seconds to two minutes at a time, then rise slowly.
- **Abdominal tightening:** Strengthen and tone the abdominal muscles. Sit up with your hands on your abdomen. Breathe in allowing your abdomen to bulge. As you breathe out, gradually tighten your abdominal muscles by pulling in your abdomen towards your backbone until your lungs are empty. Repeat this 2-3 times.
- **Pelvic tilt:** Strengthens the abdominal muscles, improves posture and relieves backaches. Lie on your back with your knees bent and feet flat on the floor. Flatten the small of your back onto the floor by contracting the abdominal muscles five times.
- **Pelvic rocking:** Move on your hands and knees, keeping your back straight.
- **Leg sliding**: Strengthen the lower abdominal muscles. Lie on your back with knees bent and feet flat on the floor. Put your hand beneath the small of your back. Maintain a pelvic tilt with your lower back flat against your, hand while slowly sliding your feet straightening both legs until you feel your low back come up.
- **Stretching:** This helps to increase the flexibility and promotes comfort during pregnancy and childbirth. Sit on the floor with your knees bent and soles of your feet together. Lean forward from your hips, relaxing your legs. Allow the weight of your legs to stretch the muscles of the inner thighs, outer thighs and buttocks gently pressing your knees towards the floor. Repeat this exercise for three to four times.
- **Hamstring stretch:** Stretch the hamstring muscles (at the back of the thighs) to help relieve backaches. Sit on the floor extending your left leg straight out. Touch your left foot with both hands keeping your back straight. Repeat on the other leg.
- **Calf stretch:** Stretch the tendons and muscles of the calf and ankle. Slowly and gently bend your front knee, putting your weight onto the front leg keeping the back straight. Hold for 30-60 seconds. Then repeat on the other leg. Repeat the process 3-4 times.

What are the necessary pre-natal examinations a pregnant woman should undertake?

Prenatal examinations or care help assure a painless delivery and the birth of a healthy baby. The following tests and examinations are performed at the prenatal visits:

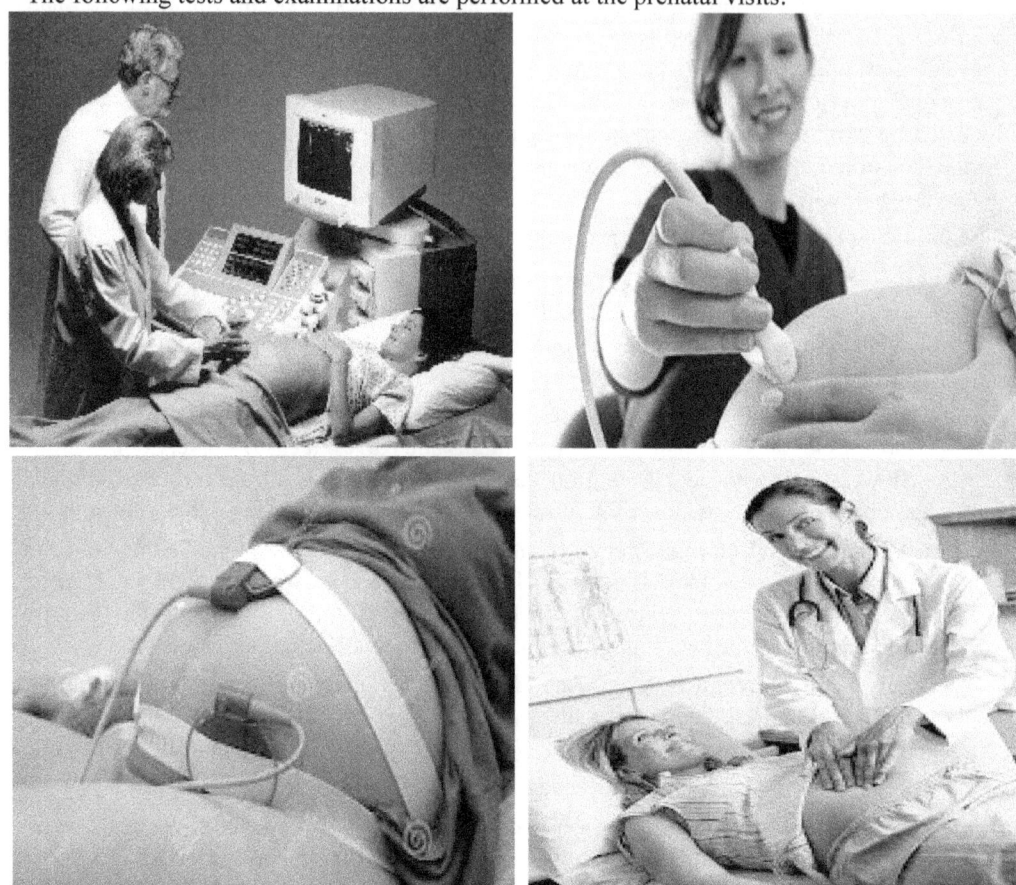

Prenatal examinations

- ▶ A complete medical history and physical examination of the expectant mother.
- ▶ A pelvic (vaginal) examination to estimate the size and shape of your pelvis to confirm the status of pregnancy and to test for any venereal disease, such as *syphilis* and *gonorrhoea*.
- ▶ A complete blood test to determine the blood type, Rh factor, check for anaemia, blood sugar, infection and German measles immunity.
- ▶ Weight check, blood pressure, urine test and diabetes.
- ▶ Abdominal examination to measure the growth of the uterus, growth of the foetus and estimate the size and position of the foetus.

I always feel depressed during this last month of pregnancy, suggest.

Remember, *depression* is common among pregnant women as well as after the childbirth, which causes a woman not only to lose sexual and other interests, besides feeling irritability and fatigue most of the time. The depression is more likely to occur if a woman feels isolated and there is inadequate support from her husband and other members of her family. During this period of pregnancy and after the delivery, the mother should pay visits to the doctor for regular check ups, which gives the mother the opportunity to discuss any problem faced by her.

The following natural remedies are suggested:
- ▶ Sunlight: Body needs sunlight. The lack of sunlight can disturb the production of key hormones and brain chemicals triggering depression.
- ▶ Very light exercise, it is must to reduce depression.
- ▶ Light music: Music lifts depression.

Losing figure due to excessive accumulation of flesh around the tummy in the 8th and 9th month, can you advise?

You have started gaining weight, and your tummy has put on extra flesh because of your skin and

Third Timester of Pregnancy

your muscles must have grown to hold the constant weight of the baby in womb. Do not worry, the muscles gradually start tightening up again sometime after the childbirth. Do not forget to undertake gentle exercises during pregnancy after consulting your doctor. Breastfeeding helps the stomach to get back to shape as it helps the uterus to contract and within two months after the delivery, the uterus takes a non-pregnant size.

Suggest how to plan for a healthy child.

Remember, a child's health does not start after the birth, it begins even before the baby conceives in the mother's womb. Planning of a child must be considered in three factors:

Before conception, during conception and after conception during the period of pregnancy. Oral contraceptives have harmful side effects and are not advised.

Start treatment under the *Acupressure Therapy* at least three months prior to conceiving in the following ways:

- ▶ The couple should take a glass of charged water (health drink) daily.
- ▶ The female partner must have three regular menses before conceiving to have a healthy fully developed uterus.
- ▶ A daily massage on both sides of the wrists for five minutes by the female partner proves beneficial for a healthy pregnancy.

To prepare charged water (health drink), mix 300 gm. of Amla powder to 100 gm. ginger powder. Swallow one teaspoonful of this powder with water in the morning and evening.

Another way is to add two teaspoonful of the above powder of Amla and ginger in four glasses of water. Use fresh Amla and ginger (if available). Boil the mixture, till it is reduced to three glasses.

Filter the liquid and add to it salt or honey to your taste. Amla is a concentrated form of vitamin C. It has 16 times more vitamin C than lemon and helps to provide protection to the body against cold, and increases the digestive power. Health drink is beneficial, especially for the convalescing people, old, growing children and the expectant mothers.

What is the effect of childbirth in the 8th month?

Mostly an *infant born in the 8th month doesn't survive.* A 30 years old woman gave birth to a baby, which did not survive beyond 16 hours. Her second child too was born premature and died within 24 hours. Many natural salts including calcium are needed for the healthy growth of a child in the womb.

If the diet of an expecting mother is deficient in these salts, the foetus doesn't develop normally and the mother may suffer from weakness of muscles, which support the uterus and may have a miscarriage.

Even if the delivery is normal, the child more often is sickly and too weak. *Calcium is found in leafy vegetables and milk in abundant quantities* and if an expecting mother takes a diet containing ample quantities of nutrients, she will deliver a healthy baby. She must seek the advice of a doctor.

Is breast tumour or cancer common during pregnancy? What are the various types of cancers and what precautions are required?

No. A woman should consult a doctor on finding an abnormality in breast or cervix.

The following types of cancers are common in women:

Breast Tumour and Cancer: This is very common in women of every age. If there is only one single nodule or lump in the breasts, painful or without pain, it should always be removed. In case the cancer appears to have extended into the neighbouring lymph nodes, the patient should be given extensive radiation therapy. Majority of breast cancers occur in either the upper portion of the breast, towards the shoulder or close to the nipple. *Breast cancer is more common in women between the age of 35 to 65 years.* It may also occur in teenage girls.

Cancer in the Cervix: This is a vicious killer of woman today. Every female after the age of 18 should have a Pelvic Examination and a *Pap smear*, at least once a year or after six months. Any pain in the lower belly or a water discharge should be investigated, as it could be a *cancer*. Be careful, if the bleeding or spotting follows intercourse or douching. Modern treatment for the uterine cancer consists of implanting a small amount of *radium* within the cervical canal followed later by heavy dose of *radiation therapy* to the whole area. Performing a *hysterectomy*, removing the uterus, cervix, ovaries and tubes are the common treatments performed when suffering from a cervical cancer.

Cancer in the Uterus: This is a less common type of cancer, known as *fundal carcinoma*. It may sometimes develop within the cavity of the uterus itself. This is less malignant than cancer of the cervix and can be detected by *Pap smear*. If cancer is found, a hysterectomy should be done without delay. The cancer cells find their way into the abdominal cavities and may spread to the pelvis and eventually, in the whole body.

Ovarian Cysts and Cancer: It is the most frequent tumour in the body. Every woman has a small cyst on the ovary, which may disappear spontaneously. The ovarian cyst causes distension of the abdomen and pressure on the organs, such as the bladder or the *rectum*. It should be removed by surgery without delay. Cancer may develop in the wall of the ovarian cyst, and spread to other nearby organs causing *obstruction of the bowel*.

What are the common problematic deliveries?

Surgical Delivery: Usually, if the foetal head is stuck higher up, a cesarean delivery is needed and surgery is required. Cesarean section should not be the last resort of the obstetrician after other methods of delivery have been attempted and have failed. Today, cesarean birth is a relatively safe, surgical operation in which the baby is born through the incision in the uterine and abdominal walls instead of through the vagina. An incision is made horizontally at the lower part of the abdomen and the baby and placenta are removed through a cut in the uterus and the abdomen, closed by stitching. In an emergency delivery, the baby is removed out by a long vertical cut. *A cesarean birth may be indicated for the following reasons:*

- ▶ **Pelvic disproportion**: A space problem resulting from a large baby or a small pelvic structure or a combination of the two.
- ▶ **Mal-presentation**: When the baby is situated unfavourably for a vaginal birth.
- ▶ **A prolonged labour**: Often, when the contractions are of poor quality or the dilation and descent are not progressing.
- ▶ **Foetal distress**: Due to changes in the foetal heart rate when the baby's oxygen supply has been reduced.
- ▶ **Prolapsed cord**: It occurs when the umbilical cord descends through the vagina before the baby is delivered resulting reduced oxygen supply.

- ▶ **Placenta previa**: When the placenta covers the cervix. As the cervix dilates, the placenta separates from the uterus depriving the foetus of oxygen.
- ▶ **Abruption of placenta**: When the placenta prematurely separates from the uterine wall.
- ▶ **Maternal disease**: If the mother has *toxemia, diabetes, high blood pressure, heart disease* or other conditions, she or her baby may not be able to withstand the stress of labour and vaginal birth.
- ▶ **Repeat cesarean**: Sometimes, it is planned in advance because the original problem still exists or there may be a risk of uterine rupture.
- ▶ **Heart disease in pregnancy**: Every attempt must be made to avoid cesarean section in these cases. A cardiac patient is not a suitable candidate for trial labour.

Complications: An incision is made in the middle line of the abdominal wall, about six inches in length. Just before incising the uterus, it is desirable to give 0.25 mg. of methergine (strictly as advised by the doctor) intravenously directly into the uterine muscle to promote the efficient *uterine contraction and retraction*. The suturing of the uterine incision immediately after the baby is delivered and this helps to control the haemorrhage. The placenta should be expressed by pressing the fundus and pushing out the placenta through the incision in the uterine. Care should be taken before the delivery of the head to see that the incision is sufficiently long to allow the head to pass out comfortably.

Ectopic or Tubal Pregnancy: It is a rare complication in which the fertilized ovum or embryo becomes blocked in its passage through the Fallopian Tube. The embryo continues to grow as it normally would within the uterus. However, the space within the tube is too small to allow expansion, which may rupture causing a serious haemorrhage. *Ectopic pregnancy is one of the leading causes of maternal death, with severe pain, abnormal vaginal bleeding and a palpable adnexal mass present in most of the patients.* The factors increasing the risk of ectopic pregnancy include:

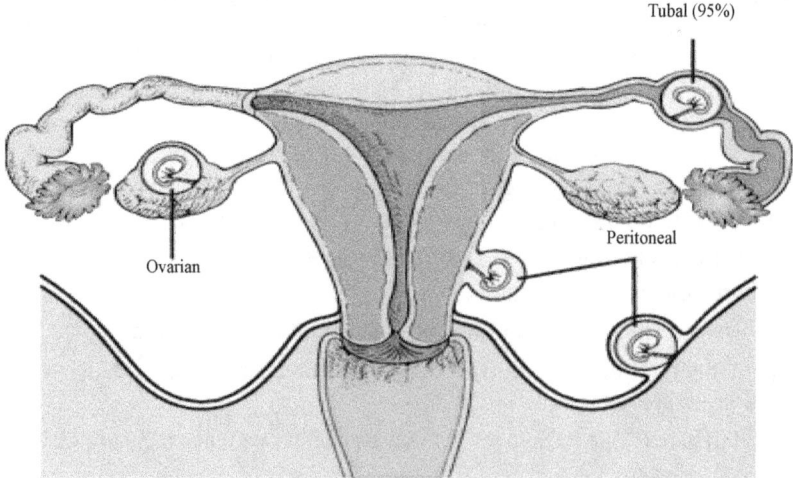

Ectopic or Tubal Pregnancy

- ► Tubal abnormality resulting in delayed transit
- ► Previous tubal pregnancy
- ► Previous history of tubal reconstructive surgery
- ► Intrauterine contraceptive devices and factors, such as increased age and parity.

Induced Delivery: In this delivery, labour is brought on or induced artificially by rupturing the membranes and letting out a little amniotic fluid, which stimulates labour pain. When the pain is too feeble or the delivery is overdue, labour is induced through medicines to contract the uterus.

Premature Delivery: The termination of pregnancy after the foetus becomes visible, such as capable of living independently is called *premature birth*. If the foetus is born dead, it is still-birth. Causes of *abortion* can also endanger the growth of the foetus resulting in a still-born or *premature delivery*. Premature birth is usually the problem with the placenta and the faulty blood supply to the foetus, defective hormone production and effects of injurious toxins and chemicals through the blood to the foetus.

Chapter 5

Three Stages of Labour

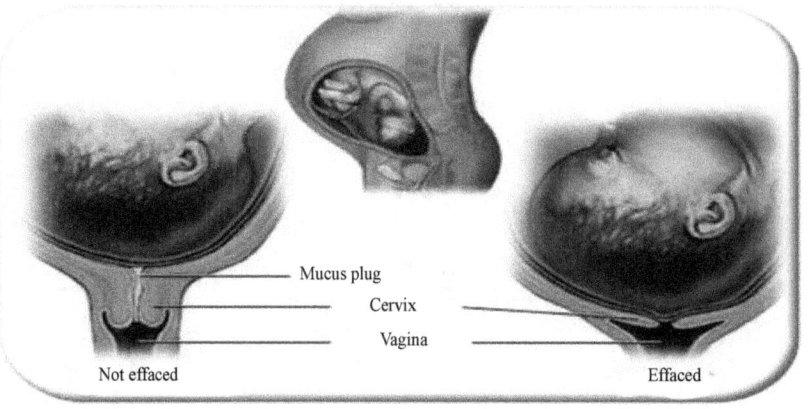

Labour Pain & Childbirth

During labour, *the uterus contracts,* the *cervix thins and opens, and the mother gives birth to the baby.* The placenta, the umbilical cord and the amniotic sac, in fact, the entire process of childbirth usually takes from a *few hours to a day or more* in the transition to parenthood for the woman.

Labour is the climax of pregnancy, when many seemingly separate systems work in harmony to bring about birth. *Dilation refers to the opening of the cervix* slightly before the onset of labour, which is estimated during a vaginal examination and is measured in centimeters. When the cervix is opened only a fingertip, it is one centimetre dilated and it is five centimetres at halfway point. When fully dilated, it is 10 centimetres dilated.

Labour usually has four stages: The first stage is called the *dilating stage* during which the cervix opens completely. The second stage is known as the *expulsion stage* or the actual birth and begins when the cervix is fully dilated and ends when the baby is born. The third stage is *the placental stage* after the birth of the baby with the delivery of the placenta. The fourth stage is known as the *recovery stage,* which begins after the placenta is born and ends to several hours after the delivery of the baby and the mother's condition stabilizes.

What are the common types of labour?

The following are the common types of labours, each having three stages:

Precipitate labour: A precipitate labour lasts less than three hours. A precipitate labour is sometimes so quick and uneventful that a pregnant woman misses even the early signs of labour. If a hospital birth has been planned, leave the home quickly, trying to cope with strong, late labour contractions. If the pregnant is unaware that her labour is progressing rapidly and thinks she is in early labour with very painful contractions, she may feel unprepared, discouraged, would feel loneliness and a lack of direction, panic and unsure of her ability to handle labour.

- In the initial stage, a woman should take deep, slow and relaxing breaths. Have a thorough vaginal examination before taking any decision about anesthesia.
- When the second stage begins, lie on your side rather than using a gravity-assisted position, which will give your birth canal and perineum more time to stretch, decrease the likelihood of tearing and protect the baby's head from being pressed through the vagina.

Prolonged labour: A labour that lasts longer than 24 hours is considered a *prolonged labour*. A labour with a long pre-labour or long latent phase can discourage, exhaust and emotionally drain the mother. On the other hand, a labour that slows or stops in the active phase or later may be complicated and is called a complicated labour.

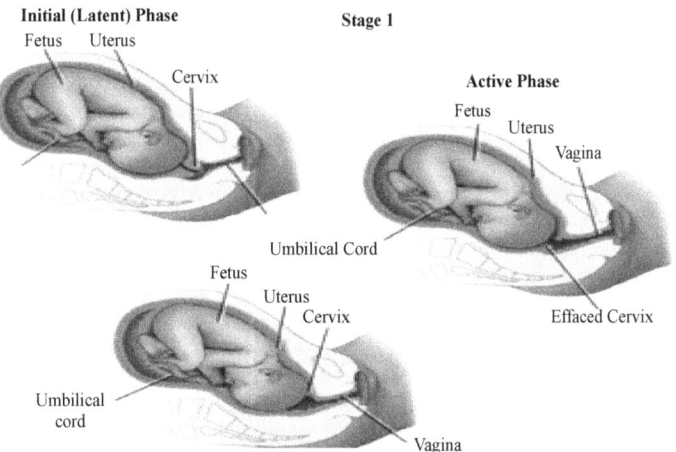

Prolonged Labour

Emergency delivery: You may find it very disturbing if you had arranged your delivery in a hospital, and you have to change your plans to have the baby at home. Don't panic, it is better to stay home than to attempt to rush to the hospital. The following suggestions will help you to maintain control of an emergency situation and ensure the best possible results.

The following are the signs of an imminent birth:

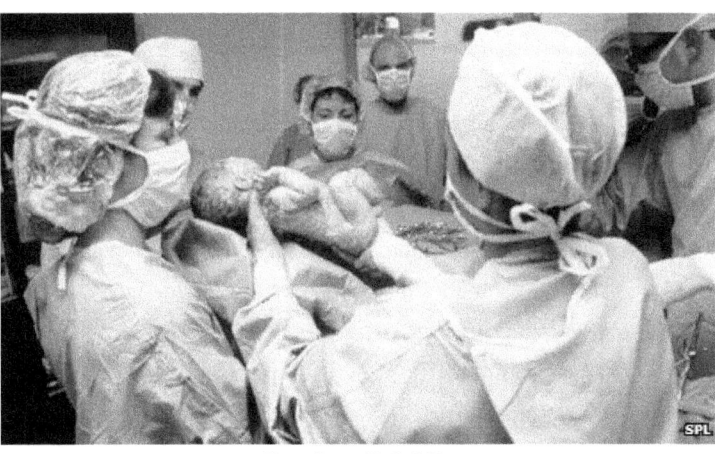

Ectopic or Tubal Pregnancy

- Feeling of a strong urge to bear down.
- The baby's head or presenting part is visible at the vagina.

- ▶ Feeling of the baby coming out.

Call someone to help you - your partner, a relative, a neighbour or a friend. You should immediately follow the following routine:

- ▶ Remove clothes from the lower half of the expectant mother's body.
- ▶ Lie on the side or in a semi-sitting position in a warm, comfortable place, preferably on the bed with a waterproof sheet, clean towels or folded linen under the buttocks.
- ▶ Stay as relaxed as possible. Let the uterus do the work. Try not to push or bear down with the contractions. Keep tissues, clean towels and blankets nearby.
- ▶ During the birth, when the baby's scalp is seen at the vagina, it will be wet and somewhat wrinkled, and it may be streaked with blood in places. The pressure of the baby's head bulges the perineum and the anus. With the contractions, more and more baby's head is visible. As the baby's head descends, the expectant mother should expel the contents of her lower bowel. She must keep her thighs and pelvic floor relaxed. If the baby's head is delivered slowly, it lessens the risk of tearing the perineum.
- ▶ Once the head is fully emerged from the vagina, the partner or the attendant should use a clean handkerchief to wipe away excess mucus from around the baby's nose and mouth, and wipe the baby's face thoroughly. With the next contractions, the expectant mother delivers the shoulders and the rest of the body smoothly. Your partner or attendant can support the baby's wet and slippery body as it emerges.

What are the common symptoms just before the delivery?

Every expecting mother should be familiar with the symptoms as the time of confinement nears. At the time of childbirth, a woman requires lots of love, affection and confidence from her husband and family members to overcome the pain barrier.

The following symptoms are observed just before a delivery:

- ▶ The sudden onset of labour pain is brought on by the drop in the level of the progesterone hormone.
- ▶ There is an urge for frequent urination.
- ▶ The low position of the foetal head makes walking and sitting difficult.
- ▶ There is backache and tiredness in the limbs.
- ▶ Vaginal secretion increases; it may be blood-stained.
- ▶ The abdomen goes into regular, periodic tightness due to uterine contractions.

What are the essential post-partum care of the child and the mother?

- ▶ The Newborn needs 10 to 20 hours sleep.
- ▶ Touching, cuddling and skin contact required.
- ▶ The Uterine is at the height of the navel after the birth and returns to the pre-pregnant location and size by 10 days of post-partum.
- ▶ After - pains in the uterus are common and there is no need to worry.
- ▶ Urination and perspiration increases.

- Lochia (vaginal flow) is present.
- Breasts enlarge in case of breastfeeding.
- Fatigue and excitement exist.
- Weight loss may be 6 to 8 kg in early post-partum.
- The menstruation in general does not return for months if breastfeeding, otherwise periods start in 4 to 8 weeks.
- Ovulation may be delayed, but is possible within weeks.
- Sexual relationship is readjusted with contraception.

What are common prenatal examinations?

Prenatal examination or care helps assure the birth of a healthy baby.

The following tests and examinations are performed at the prenatal visits:
- A complete medical history and physical examination of the expectant mother.
- A pelvic (vaginal) examination to estimate the size and shape of your pelvis, to confirm pregnancy, to do a Pap smear to detect cervical cancer and to test for venereal disease such a syphilis and gonorrhoea.
- A complete blood test to determine your blood type, Rh factor, to test for anaemia, blood sugar, infection and German measles immunity.
- Weight check, blood pressure, urine tests for diabetes and to detect excess protein.
- Abdominal examination to measure the growth of the uterus, growth of the foetus and estimate the size and position of the foetus.

What are the common symptoms of an expectant mother just before the delivery?

Every expecting mother should be familiar with the symptoms as the time of confinement nears. At the time of childbirth, a woman requires lots of love, affection and confidence from her husband and family members to overcome the pain barrier.

The following symptoms are observed just before a delivery:
- The sudden onset of labour pain is brought on by the drop in the level of the progesterone hormone.
- There is an urge for frequent urination.
- The low position of the foetal head makes walking and sitting difficult.
- There is backache and tiredness in the limbs.
- Vaginal secretion increases; and it may be blood-stained.
- The abdomen goes into regular, periodic tightness due to uterine contractions.

Motherhood ....Through a Year of Pregnancy

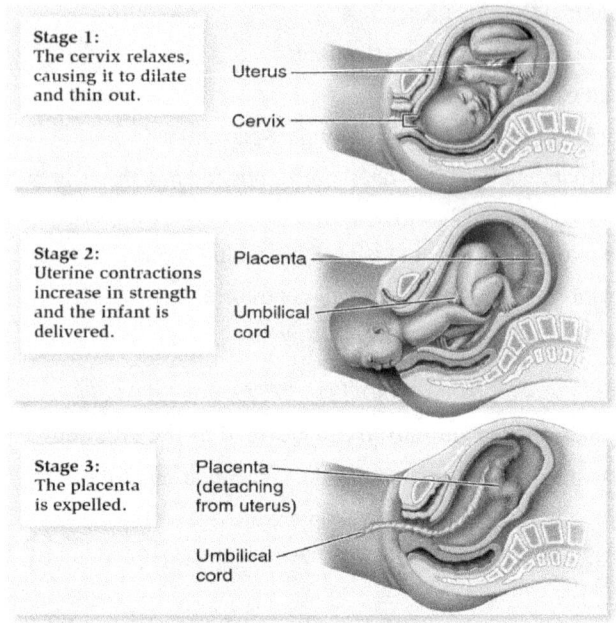

Common Stages of Labour

What are the common stages of labour?

Labour is divided into *three stages,* besides the *final stage also known as the recovery stage* as follows:

- ▶ **First Stage-The Dilating Stage:** During this stage, the cervix opens completely.
- ▶ **Second Stage-The Expulsion Stage:** Also called actual birth, which begins when the cervix is fully dilated and ends when the baby is born.
- ▶ **Third Stage-The Placental Stage:** Begins with the birth of the baby and ends with the delivery of the placenta.
- ▶ **Fourth Stage-The Recovery Stage:** This begins after the placenta is born and ends on to several hours later when the mother's condition stabilizes.

Dilation and signs of labour

When the *gestation period* is over, the mother is about to deliver the child, and the expecting mother begins getting *severe labour pain.* Usually the types of women feel less pain during delivery are those accustomed to domestic work, do regular morning and evening walk, undertake regular exercise and have sound health and possess well-developed pelvis.

Dilation refers to the opening of the cervix. It is usual for the cervix to dilate slightly before the onset of labour. The dilation is estimated during a vaginal examination and is measured in centimetres. When the cervix is opened only a fingertip, it is one centimetre dilated, and at the halfway point, it is four to five centimetres. When fully dilated, it is eight to ten centimetres dilated. The prominent signs of labour are the following:

What are the common signs of labour?

- ▶ Backache, that come and go accompanied by uneasiness and restlessness.

Three Stages of Labour

Common Signs of Labour

- ▶ Frequent soft bowel movements often mistaken for an intestinal upset. Diarrhoea-like symptoms on or near your due date may be a subtle sign of early labour.
- ▶ Passage of a thickened mucus plug tinged with blood from the ruptured blood vessels in the cervix, which can appear days before any other sign of labour.
- ▶ Contractions of the uterus become longer, stronger and closer together as labour advances. Contractions usually become painful near the delivery period. The uterine contractions shorten the muscle fibres in the body of the uterus, pull open the cervix and push the foetus down and out of the uterus.
- ▶ Rupture of the membranes or breaking of the bag of water begins labour usually immediately, or within 24 hours. When the membranes break, followed by a gush of amniotic fluid, sometimes it is very slow, uncontrollable leak of fluid and the patient may feel like urination. When the rupture of membrane occurs and labour doesn't begin, the risk of infection increases as time passes. Seek medical advice and note the time, colour, odour and amount of the fluid. Do not insert anything into your vagina to control the flow. Avoid inserting fingers, having intercourse and taking a tub bath. That can increase the possibility of infection.

What are the causes of severe pain during childbirth?

There are many factors as below:

- ▶ Insufficient supply of oxygen to the uterine muscles. The pain is more intense if the interval between contractions is short.

- ▶ Stretching of the cervix.
- ▶ Pressure by the baby on the nerves near the cervix and vagina.
- ▶ Tension on and stretching of the supporting ligaments of the uterus and the surrounding structures during pregnancy.
- ▶ Pressure on the urethra, bladder and the rectum.
- ▶ Distention of the pelvic floor muscles.
- ▶ Fear and anxiety, which release excess stress hormones.

How to examine the pelvic region of an expectant woman before labour?

The objects are two-fold: to investigate the condition of the pelvic organs and to estimate the size and shape of the pelvic canal. It is necessary to measure the pelvis by your doctor by means of a *bimanual examination*. The diagnosis of pregnancy is confirmed and the presence or absence of the pelvic swellings, such as *uterine fibroids* or *ovarian cysts can* be determined. If the fundus (top of the uterus) can be palpated abdominally, there is no need to carry out the pelvic examination at the first visit and can be postponed until need arises. *There are three methods of pelvic examination, as mentioned below:*

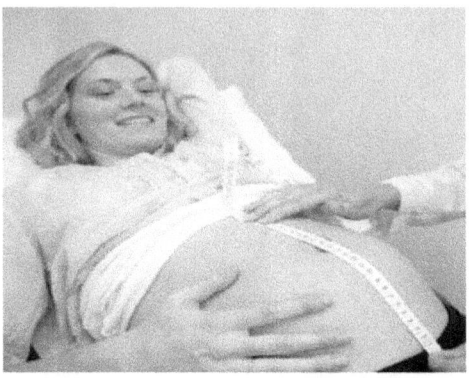
Doctor Examining the Pelvic Region of a Pregnant Lady

1. **External Examination:** The measurements are made with a pair of calipers to find out any deformity.

2. **Internal Examination:** The internal diameter is measured with hands. The two, anterior-superior spines are located, where fingers are placed on their outer lips and the measurement read off. Normally, it is 24 –25 cm. in an average pregnant. The internal diameter is also measured around the *iliac cresta*, which is normally 26-27 cm.

3. **By X-rays:** The size of the pelvis and the foetal head can be assessed by an X-ray. This process is also known as *Radiographic Pelvimetry*.

How to prepare for delivery?

One must keep the following things ready before delivery:
- ▶ A hard bed to avoid excess labour pain.
- ▶ Oily cloth for spreading on the bed.
- ▶ Two rolls of sterilised cotton wool.
- ▶ Few napkins duly rinsed in carbolic lotion and dried.
- ▶ Two basins, each for membranes and waste cotton.
- ▶ Enema pot, boric acid and antiseptic lotion.
- ▶ Four binders of size 36" long and 16" broad for stomach which is required immediately after the delivery.
- ▶ Four loin clothes to manage the vagina.

Three Stages of Labour

What are some of the essentials just before and after the delivery?

Labour is divided into three stages, as described below:

- ▶ The first stage lasts about 12-15 hours.
- ▶ The second stage about two hours.
- ▶ The third stage takes 20 minutes to half an hour.

In the patients belonging to working class, the average time is considerably shorter. The first stage occupies 8-10 hours, the second stage one hour or less, and the third stage 20 minutes to half an hour. These are average figures and the labour class women usually complete their labour in a much shorter time.

Explain the various stages of delivery.

Stage of dilation (The first stage of labour): It starts from the onset of true pain to the full dilation of the cervix. The occurrence includes periodic pain due to contraction of the uterus with a hardening of the organ, which can be felt by the hands placed on the abdomen. There is a continuous discharge from the vagina and known as 'show'. As the pain becomes more frequent

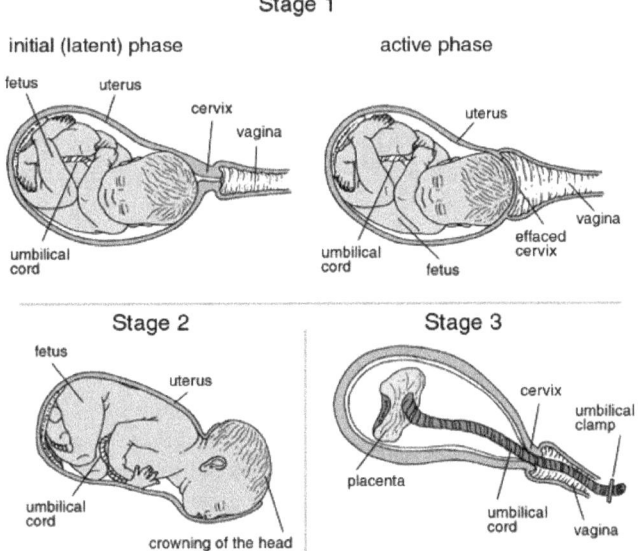

Various Stages of Delivery

and severe, the patient begins to cry out and feels relief by sitting bent forward. A gentle massage on the back from shoulder to the lower back is also helpful for the patient to relieve tension. It takes 12 to 15 hours to complete the first stage. At the end of it, there is usually a sudden gush of fluid indicating that the foetal membranes have ruptured.

The cervix dilation varies from 8 to 10 cm. with strong contractions and heavy pressure on the vagina and the rectum. The delivering woman feels nausea, vomiting or vomiting sensation, drowsiness, hiccups, cold feet, uncontrollable shaking and frequent leg cramps. There is always a possibility of rupture of the membranes. The expectant mother feels restless, irritable, forgetful, fearful, often a controlled urge to push and have difficulty in breathing. A pregnant woman at this stage should not be left alone. Back rubbing provides comfort.

Stage of expulsion (The second stage of labour): This is a stage of expulsion and extends from the complete dilation of the cervix to the expulsion of the child. The pain often stops for few minutes after the rupture and then again begins with greater frequency, which gradually become more expulsive or 'downbearing' in character. The patient usually braces herself by holding on to some solid object or pressing her feet against the foot of the bed. The diaphragm is thus fixed and the intra-abdominal pressure brought to bear on the expulsion of the child. The patient perspires freely. The effect of this pain is to drive the head through the cavity of the pelvis. It presses upon the rectum and on the perineum, which begins to bulge a little during the pain. The vulva also begins to gape more.

Gradually, the pain becomes longer and more frequent, the head recedes a little, but with each succeeding pain, it is driven a little farther down. The perineum bulges more and more, the vulva too gapes more and more and the scalp of the baby is seen when the head is forced down during pain. Larger and larger area of the head comes to lie in the vulva opening during successive pains. The opening becomes transformed from a slightly gaping slit to an oval and ultimately an almost circular opening. The perineum in the meantime has been so pressed that it becomes stretched out and thinned. After the head is born, there is a short pause during which the face of the child becomes congested. After the head, the shoulders, the trunk and the lower limbs are pushed out, followed by a gush of the remainder of the liquid. After the end of the second stage, the retracted uterus may be felt as a firm tumour extending up to just below the umbilicus.

The expectant mother has possible full contractions in this stage when the urge to push becomes stronger due to the pressure of the stretching vagina and physical signs of birth of the baby's head, and then the body. The mother must relax the perineum, buttocks, legs and change position for comfort as necessary. Remove the clothing from the lower half of the body. Lie on the side or in semi-sitting position in a warm, comfortable place with clean towels or folded linen under the buttocks. A waterproof sheet will protect the mattress. Stay as relaxed as possible.

Stage of Delivery (The third stage of labour): This is the stage of delivery of the child and extends from the birth of the child to the birth of the placenta. There is usually a short cessation of pain with a corresponding relief to the patient. Ultimately, the uterus begins to contract again, and may be felt by the hand to grow more hard and solid. Sometimes, there are little gushes of blood during the pain, indicating the separation of the placenta. Many times, there is no bleeding. In the end, the placenta is expelled out by strong pain in the vagina. The third stage may take a few minutes to an hour or even more. The average time is about 15-20 minutes.

In this stage, *the breathing pattern should be slow or accelerated breathing.* The pregnant woman may try to push to expel the placenta. There are mild to moderate contractions and uncontrollable shaking during this period. Excitement, fatigue and engrossment with the baby are possible emotional signs, an expectant mother may experience. The mother should push the placenta out as directed and hold the baby skin to skin. When you first see the baby's scalp at the vagina, it will be wet and wrinkled and may be streaked with blood. The pressure of the baby's head bulges the perineum and the anus. If the head is delivered slowly, it lessens the risk of tearing the perineum. Keep the thighs and the pelvic floor relaxed as the head emerges from the vagina. Once the head has fully emerged, the attendant should use a clean handkerchief to wipe away the excess mucus from around the baby's nose and mouth. If the cord is around the baby's neck, the attendant should lift it gently over the baby's head.

Usually the baby begins breathing and crying immediately. Place the baby on the side on the bare abdomen with head slightly lower than the body to drain any mucus remaining on the face. Wipe away any mucus and dry the baby completely. Keep the baby warm. Remember, contractions will resume when the placenta separates from the uterine wall and slide down into the vagina. A mother can start breastfeeding right away, which will stimulate the uterus to contract and reduce bleeding. If the uterus is not firm, massage the fundus (top of the uterus) until it contracts. *In case the newly born baby does not breathe spontaneously, rub his/her back or chest briskly, but gently. If it doesnot respond within 30 seconds, hold the baby's feet together and smack the soles sharply. If still doesn't respond, then mouth to mouth resuscitation is required by placing the mouth over the baby's nose and mouth and blowing air gently in the cheeks until the chest rises a little.*

How should the placenta be separated?

The resumption of pain after the birth of the child indicates still further contraction and retraction of the upper segment. This brings about such a disproportion between the placental site and the placenta when the attachments between the two are torn through. The placental site may be reduced in area 4-1/2 by 4 inches (11 by 10 cm.) without separation taking place.

There are two methods of expulsion of the placenta:

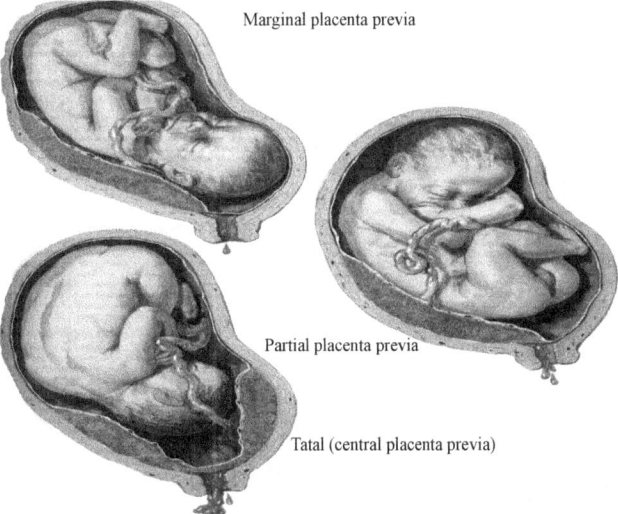

Separation of the Placenta

- ▶ **Schultze's method:** This is the process in which the placenta is expelled like an inverted umbrella when the foetal surface comes first and the membrane trailing behind.

- ▶ **Dubcan's mechanism:** Its also known as the *Matthews Duncan*. In it, the lower edge of the placenta is first extruded, and the whole organ slides downfolded longitudinally upon it. This method is more common.

What is the fourth stage of delivery?

The first hours after birth is known as the *fourth stage* in which the delivered mother must breathe slowly and is also known as *the Recovery Stage*. This is the stage when the just delivered mother feels shaking, have after-pains (painful uterine contractions), perineal discomforts, fatigue, exhaustion, empty feeling, difficulty while urination, hunger and nausea. She has the desire to see and hold the baby. Rest and relaxation are important factors at this stage. She must drink or eat, urinate in sitting up position, massage fundus and apply ice pack to the perineum to decrease discomfort and swelling.

How to control haemorrhage soon after the delivery?

As the placenta is separated from the wall of the uterus, the blood vessels passing from the one to the other are torn across, and many of the large sinuses in the uterine wall thus laid open. Bleeding from these is, however, prevented by the very retraction of the uterus, which causes the separation. If owing to exhaustion of the uterus, retraction fails to occur after the separation of the placenta, then free and alarming bleeding may take place – known as the *pos-partum haemorrhage.*

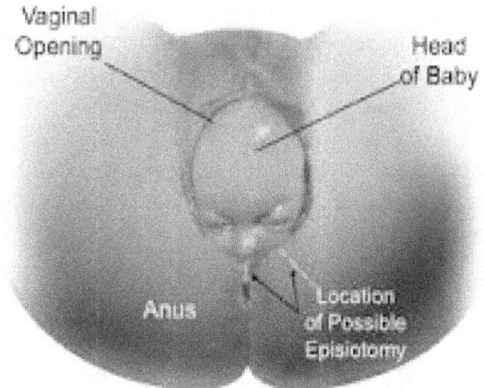

Crowning and Episiotomy

Fourth Stage of Delivery

Some bleeding will occur *after labour and delivery*. If there is blood loss more than two cups, the mother may be haemorrhaging characterising by a steady flow of blood and symptoms of shock with rapid pulse, paleness, trembling, cold and sweating are seen. On suspecting haemorrhage, firmly massage the uterus through the abdominal wall until it contracts. If the bleeding appears to ooze from the tears at the vaginal opening, pad the perineum with an ice pack and towels.

Remember, *vaginal secretion* in a healthy pregnancy differs only in its increased quantity from that of a healthy non-pregnant woman. It is whitish in colour containing epithelial cells, leucocytes, mucus and numerous large 'vaginal bacilli'.

How to clean the genitals after labour?

Nature follows the *principles of antisepsis* in labour. *The birth canal can be divided into three parts:*

- ▶ **The vulva (the entrance to the vagina):** This area swarms with organisms of various sorts. It may therefore be designated as the *Septic tract.*
- ▶ **The vagina:** The portion containing the vaginal bacilli with their acid secretion, a few fungi, and some leucocytes. This is the *Antiseptic tract.*
- ▶ **The cavity of the uterus:** Separated by the plug of the mucus from the vagina, is entirely devoid of any form of organism. It is therefore the *Aseptic tract.*

Wherever possible, the patient should have a complete bath at the very commencement of labour, and the nurse should see that the rectum and the bladder are emptied. It is usually suggested that the patient should be given an enema in every case, irrespective of whether the bowels have acted naturally or not. The nurse should then pay special attention to the genitals. The hair around the vaginal area should be shaved. Before a vaginal examination is made, the vulva is swabbed with an antiseptic solution. The *labia minora* must be separated and wiped with wool soaked in an antiseptic solution. The pledget must be used not more than one wipe always and be drawn from being backwards to prevent carrying forward any septic matter from near the anus.

What is puerperal infection?

Puerperal infection is described as an infection during or after the labour, generally applied to the uterus and the surrounding tissues after delivery. This can vary from mild to life threatening in severity. Some of the most severe infections may appear within hours of the delivery and are often opportunistic and non-associated with reliable risk factors. Vigilance and aggressive diagnosis and treatment are required. The puerperal infection is causesd due to colonisation and infection of the tissues of the uterus, the peritoneum or the surrounding organs. *Abscesses* usually contain both *aerobic and anaerobic bacteria.* Nearly 50 percent of the ascending uterine infections involve harmful bacteria due to lack of cleanliness. The risk factors of this infection includes a cesarean delivery, invasive procedure during labour, prolonged rupture of the membranes, prolonged labour, multiple examinations, retained placental fragments, urinary catheter, intravenous line(s), low socio-economic status and chronic diseases including diabetes.

The signs and symptoms of the infection are fever after delivery, uterine tenderness, sign of septic or cardiovascular shock, hypertension, anxiety, disorientation, prostration, impaired renal function, haemolysis or haemo-concentration.

The infection can be diagnosed by the following symptoms:
- Urinary tract infection with the presence of large numbers of White Blood Cells (WBCs)
- Wound infection
- Infection in the intravenous line or site and contaminated fluids
- Disturbed abscess
- Septic thrombophlebitis, necrotising fasciitis, transfusion reaction, amniotic fluid or pulmonary embolism
- Cardiogenic shock and toxic shock syndrome
- Mastitis and afelectasis
- Possible associated conditions, such as septic shock, adult respiratory distress syndrome, acute renal failure and disseminated intravascular coagulation

Prenatal infections, especially *neonatal bacterial sepsis* is the commonest cause of *neonatal mortality in India* in which the foetus may get infected in-utero and during passage through the birth canal during pregnancy and after birth. The following infections are common:

Intrauterine Infection: It occurs due to viruses and sometimes by bacteria causing diseases, such as *syphilis, tuberculosis, malaria, varicella, Hepatitis B, Coxsackie B, HIV, Rubella, Herpes Simplex,* etc.

Cytomegalic: About 60 to 70% patients may suffer from bleeding, anaemia, interstitial pneumonia and deafness, due to this infection.

Rubella: About 60 to 70% patients suffer from bleeding, which may cause retardation, retinitis with pigmentation, congenital cardiac defects, valvular pulmonic stenosis, deafness and glaucoma.

Toxoplasmosis: It causes severe anaemia due to bleeding.

Congenital Syphilis: It causes rashes and snuffles, depressed nasal bridge periosteitis and chondrites.

Herpes Virus: This causes vesicles and pneumonia and herpes genitalia in mother.

Coxsackie B: IT causes respiratory distress due to carditis.

Congenital Malaria: It occurs due to administering infected blood.

Bacterial Infection: It causes blood infection, umbilical cord and ear and throat swab

Fungal Infection (Candida): This causes oral and perineal moniliasis pneumonia.

Protozoal Infection: It causes congenital malaria.

Spirochetal Infection: It causes rashness, snuffles, hepatitis and periostesis.

Viral Infection: This Includes cytomegalo virus, herpes virus, vericella-zostar (chicken pox herpes zoster) influenza, measles and mumps, which may cause vesicles, throat swab, hepatitis, anaemia, deafness, cataract and cardiac malformations.

Which are the common medical interventions during labour?

There are various interventions involved in labour and birth, which have benefits as well as risks and some of the important ones are described below:

- ▶ **Intravenous (IV) fluids:** The fluids are administered through plastic tube or needle inserted into the vein in the back of hand or in the arm when the patient is unable to drink liquids. Usually Pitocin is administered through IV for induced labour.
- ▶ **Prostaglandin:** A gel or tablet of prostaglandin is placed in the cervix for 24 hours, or at least overnight to soften the cervix and start labour causing uterine contractions. Sometimes, this intervention fails to induce labour.
- ▶ **Artificial rupture of membranes:** Before or during the process of labour, a small hole is made in the membrane with a surgical instrument for vaginal examination before starting labour, enhancing dilation and then examine the colour of amniotic liquid in the foetus. Sometimes, it increases the risk of infection and may increase the discomfort of uterine contractions.
- ▶ **Induction of labour:** A finger is inserted between the membranes and the cervix before labour begins as light bloody vaginal discharge, and is often mistaken for a bloody show. Labour may or may not begin by this intervention. However, it may cause ruptured membranes.
- ▶ **Synthetic oxytocin:** Usually, it is given in an IV to cause uterine contractions to induced labour when the membranes have ruptured. Oxytocin increases the intensity and frequency of contractions. In some cases, it may result in the incidence of jaundice in the newborn or cause premature birth.
- ▶ **Foetal stethoscope:** Used to monitor the *foetal Heart Rate (FHR)* and listening the baby's heartbeat through the abdominal wall using a stethoscope. The FHR may be counted before, during and after a contraction of about 15 to 30 minutes.
- ▶ **Episiotomy:** A surgical incision made into the perineum from the vagina towards the rectum just before the birth of the baby's head to enlarge the birth canal, speed the delivery of the baby, to provide more space for the application of forceps or vacuum extractor and reduce compression from the vaginal tissues on the head of the premature baby. *Episiotomy* causes certain disadvantages, such as discomfort in the early post-partum period, infection, frequent bleeding after delivery and pain during intercourse for several months.

- ▶ **Forceps**: A stainless steel instrument inserted into the vagina applied to each side of the baby's head to aid rotation at the time of birth of the head and helps to bring the baby down, reduce prolonged pressure in the birth canal and allow rapid delivery. Sometimes, the process may bruise the soft tissues of the baby's head or face and the vaginal tissues.
- ▶ **Vacuum extractor**: A cap like device is applied to the foetal head connected to a vacuum pump through a rubber tube to create suction on the baby's head. It requires less space and operational time, 5 to 10 minutes in the vagina and then forceps can be applied when the foetus is at a higher place. It may cause bruising or swelling of the soft scalp tissues.

Which are the vaginal examinations before delivery?

The use of *abdominal palpation is recommended.* Where a vaginal examination is necessary, it must be done with great care. The patient should lie on her back rather than on her side, so as to diminish the risk of the hand coming into contact with the anus. Cleanse your hands and the vulva before conducting the examination. The *labia minora* is separated apart by the left hand fingers. The fingers of the right hand are introduced into the vagina without coming into contact with the vulva.

Ascertain the following points during the vaginal examination:

1. State of labour; how far advanced it is?
2. Presentation and position?
3. Are the membranes ruptured?
4. State of vagina and perineum to check the rigidity, moistness or dryness.
5. Is the pelvis normal?
6. Is the cord prolapsed?

What to do in case of severe labour pains?

Prolonged Labour: A labour that lasts longer than 24 hours is called a *prolonged labour.* The more important is the phase of labour in which there are reasons for slow progress and rate of cervical dilation. A prolonged labour process can discourage, exhaust and emotionally drain or may turn to complication in an expectant mother. Do not become discouraged or depressed in case of a prolonged labour. The expectant mother should be nurtured with food or drink, bath and showers, walks and backrubs. Consult your doctor and try various methods to stimulate labour. Medical interventions are essential if the labour prolongs more than 24 hours. Stimulate effective contractions with procedures, such as stripping the membranes, administering an enema or giving drugs that ripen the cervix to induce labour.

The following steps are advised in case of prolonged labour:

- ▶ Turn by changing position every 20 to 30 minutes encouraging the baby to turn to position taking advantage of the gravity and movement.
- ▶ Stand or walk to try to align the baby's body with the entrance to the pelvis and pelvic flexibility.
- ▶ Do the pelvic rock, which may free the baby's head from the pelvis and allow it to turn to an anterior position.

▶ There is often severe back pain due to prolonged labour. To relieve back pain, prevent the baby's head from pressing on your back, apply counter-pressure on your back, ask your partner for a back massage, use hot or cold pack on your low back during or between contractions, stand or sit in the shower and let the water spray on the painful area and use pain medications, if necessary.

What to do in case of excess bleeding after the childbirth?

Mostly bleeding occurs after labour and the delivery of the baby. However, in case of loss of blood for over two cups, you may have haemorrhage with symptoms like shock, rapid pulse, paleness, trembling, cold and sweating. In case of suspected haemorrhage, massage the uterus firmly through the abdominal wall until it contracts and encourages the newly born baby to nurse besides massaging the breast nipples. If the bleeding appears at the vaginal opening, pad the perineum with an ice pack and towel. Apply firm pressure.

Chapter 6

Beautiful Body During & After Pregnancy

Diet and Body Care During Pregnancy

*Y*our eating habits before and during pregnancy affects the baby's health. Since eating properly greatly influences the growth (in the womb) and the future health of your baby. A mother should have a clear understanding of what is involved in providing the best nourishment for yourself and your unborn child.

It is never too late in pregnancy to improve your eating habits, since your baby will benefit from any improvement you make even in late pregnancy. In fact, the body's greatest need for *iron, protein* and *calcium* occurs in the last 8 to 12 weeks of pregnancy. Improving your diet will have a long-term effect on your children, since they will grow up with better eating habits. Good nutrition has important and long-lasting effects.

Food Habits during Pregnancy

During pregnancy, a woman supplies all the nutrients to the developing baby, the baby's life support system, consisting of the placenta, uterus and membranes, fluid and maternal blood volume, also grows during Pregnancy, developing as necessary to meet the increasing needs of the foetus.

Which feed and how much should a pregnant woman eat to assure the baby and herself of the best possible outcome of pregnancy? Why are these foods important? How much weight should she gain while she is pregnant? What about salt, fluid retention, special diets, heartburn, nausea and vomiting, drugs, tobacco, caffeine, herbs and other non-foods to use? For all these, should one seriously consult a doctor to get a practical advice to evaluate one's own diet?

What types of nutritious food a woman should eat during and after childbirth?

A good health depends upon the nutritive value of the diet one eats. To maintain good health, vigour and vitality during and after pregnancy, the human body needs a wide range of nutrition including proteins, fats, carbohydrates, vitamins and minerals, which are derived from the food we eat. The food we eat is classified as *cereals, pulses, legumes, nuts, oil seeds* and *grains, fruits* and *vegetables* and *milk and milk products*.

Nutritious Food for Pregnant Women

Food we eat is grouped into two parts: *nutritive*, which provides energy, heat and nutrition and *non-nutritive* that provides only energy, vitamins and minerals. *Vitamins and minerals* do not supply energy, but play a vital role in regulating the metabolic activities. Minerals help in the formation of body structure and skeleton. The role of some important nutritious substances are following:

Carbohydrates: They provide energy to the body, control the breakdown of proteins and protect them from toxins. They do burn the fat. These are found in sugar, honey, etc. Complex carbohydrates are generally found in cereals, grains, vegetables and fruits.

Proteins: These are various combinations of essential amino acids that promote growth of the body. All foods, except refined sugar, oils and fats contain proteins. Milk, oilseeds, nuts, pulses and soybean are rich source of protein, especially for the growth in infants and children, foetus development during pregnancy and helps in milk generation during lactation. An adult requires protein to the extent of 0.7 gm/kg of body weight. Children during the growing age require slightly more proteins than adults.

Fat: This is an essential part in the human body, but it is harmful if taken in excess. *Fats generally break up in the absence of carbohydrates to provide energy.* Since fat is a concentrated source of energy, any excess intake of fat accumulation is termed as *obesity*. The fat we eat consists of fatty acids, and is necessary for the growth and repair of the body. Eating too much of fat or oily food makes one obese.

Vitamins: The excess as well as shortage of vitamins, both are harmful and produce adverse effects. Some of the prominent vitamins during pregnancy are:

Vitamin A: Available in Ghee, Butter, Egg, Fish, Green Vegetables (Carrots and spinach). Deficiency causes rough and dry skin and diminished vision. Adverse effects are headaches, body aches, nausea, vomiting, itching skin and loss of hair.

Vitamin-D: Available in fish, egg, butter, milk and sun rays. Deficiency causes decreased bone growth in children, and thinning of bone in adults. Adverse effects are loss of appetite, diarrhoea, kidney failure, deposition of calcium in tissues, nervousness, trembling, headache and muscle weakness.

Vitamin B: Available in cereals, pulses, meat, dairy products, vegetables, nuts and fruits. Deficiency causes weakness and nervousness. Adverse effects are nervousness, trembling, headaches and muscle weaknesses.

Vitamin B-2: Available in most foods. Deficiency causes ulcers in the mouth, burning sensation in the eyes and scales on the skin.

Vitamin B-6: Available in meat, fish, cereals, pulses and yeast. Deficiency causes ulcers in the mouth, nerve damage and anaemia. Adverse effects are pimples, skin rashes and convulsions.

Vitamin B-12: Available in liver, fish, eggs and milk. Deficiency causes anaemia, sterility and nervous damage.

Vitamin C: Available in citrus foods, green vegetables and pulses. Deficiency causes weakness, anaemia and swelling of gums. Adverse effects are diarrhoea, kidney stone and effects on the unborn baby in the womb.

Nicotine: Available in liver, meat, fish, cereals and pulses. Deficiency causes diarrhoea, mental symptoms, ulcers in the mouth, headaches and insomnia. Adverse effects are liver damage, peptic ulcers, nausea, vomiting, diarrhoea and increase in blood sugar.

Folic acid: Available in liver, egg, leafy vegetables, etc. Deficiency causes anaemia, soreness of tongue and weakness. Adverse effects are kidney damage and insomnia.

What type of diet a woman should take during the 1st, 2nd and 3rd trimester of pregnancy and after childbirth?

The first three months of pregnancy are called the *First Trimester* and the next three months as the *Second Trimester*. During the first trimester of pregnancy, a pregnant woman shows only a few outward signs of pregnancy. The baby in the womb needs a regular supply of energy and a high quality of nutrients for its growth. It is during the first few weeks after conception that the foetus begins to form the organs and heartbeat can be detected by the second month. However, growth and maturation continues till the end of the pregnancy period. The state of mind of the mother during pregnancy affects too much over the child. Reading books, listening to music and rest makes an expectant mother happy and relaxed.

As the months roll by, the pregnant woman gets exhausted quickly. The best way to relieve tiredness and exhaustion is to ask your husband to *rub your back and shoulders as a light massage on the back muscles.* In case of severe nausea and vomiting, consult your doctor, who will prescribe an anti-vomiting drug. Intravenous glucose in a drip may be required if you are losing fluid every time you vomit. Have frequent small meals six to seven times in a day. Restrict your fluid intake in the evening to avoid frequent urination during the night. Eat hygienically cooked food. Relax for few minutes after meal. *Avoid excess of tea, coffee and smoking.*

The second trimester of pregnancy begins from the 13th week and continues up to the 28th week. The total weight gain during pregnancy should not be more than 10 to 12 kg. During the first three months, there may be little or no increase in weight. At the end of this period, there may be an increase *ranging from 0.7 to 1.4 kg. or in the first 20 weeks, a total of 4 kg.* Make sure to watch your weight during each visit to your doctor for check up. If the weight is less than the normal gain, it indicates a poor growth of your baby in the womb and you must improve your diet. If the weight is more than the normal gain, the reason could be that you are taking on excess or the wrong kind of food.

Eat a well balanced diet to avoid excessive weight gain. Include foods providing fibre in the diet to avoid constipation. *Drink plenty of fluids and water, 7 to 8 glasses in a day.* Take extra *vegetables, pulses and fruits.* Avoid excessive intake of sugar, salt and spices. Avoid canned and highly processed foods and avoid eating at unhygienic places. *The average weight gain during pregnancy is 12 kg.* Out of this, *80% is the womb and its contents.* Remember, *if you are overweight, there are chances of rise in your blood pressure and blood sugar.*

During the 3rd trimester, the appetite returns and the mother as well as the baby need a nourishing and *well-balanced diet*. Here is a daily diet chart recommended during this period:

The period after the delivery is known as the *post-partum and lactation*. The term, *lactation* means the *secretion of milk by the mammary glands (breast)*. During the first few days after delivery, a cloudy fluid called *colostrum* will be secreted in place of milk. This fluid is very beneficial for the newly born baby as it contains important antibodies to protect the infant from infections and diseases. Colostrum provides adequate nutrition to the infant until the appearance of true milk after two to three days. *Breast* feeding is very important, as it helps to build a strong bond between the mother and the baby.

There is no need to panic if you do not produce a lot of milk to feed your child immediately after the delivery. It will gradually increase as you start feeding your baby more frequently. *Your state of mind along with your diet* influences the quantity of milk you produce. The quantity and quality of milk produced is not related to the size of the breast but is dependent on the *amount of diet and fluid you consume.* The more often you feed your baby, the more milk will be produced. Drink plenty of juices, milkshake, buttermilk, soups and water. *Have minimum four litres of fluid per day,* while you are a feeding mother. Do not fix any rigid timing to feed your baby. Your baby will let you know when he is hungry by crying out.

While breastfeeding, the feeding mother will require a lot more calories than during the pregnancy. This is because breastfeeding your baby will make you burn *3500 kcal per day.* However, you need to consume only *2400 to 2700 kcal per day* during the first six months of lactation if you are exclusively breastfeeding your baby. Most doctors recommend that you breastfeed for one year, and out of this period, your baby should exclusively be breastfed for 4 to 6 months, and then you can gradually start weaning by slowly introducing your baby to a variety of foods so that he is no longer fully dependent on your breastmilk at the end of one year. Thus during the last six months of lactation, the energy requirement will decrease to about 2250 to 2550 kcal per day.

Your diet requirement during the lactation period should be as below:

- ▶ **Protein:** 75 gm/day during the initial six months of lactation period, which will reduce to 68 gm/day after six months.
- ▶ **Fat:** It is a concentrated source of energy and one requires 45 gm/day.
- ▶ **Calcium**: It is essential for the baby's development of bones as well as for the mother. The daily requirement will be 1000 mg/day. Breast milk draws calcium from the bones in the human body.
- ▶ **Iron:** Around 30 mg/day requirement is necessary to maintain the haemoglobin level in the body that supplies oxygen to each cell of the body. *Iron deficiency leads to anaemia.*

- ▶ **Folic acid:** 150 mg/day is required for the growth and development of the brain and spine of the baby. The deficiency can also lead to anaemia in the mother.
- ▶ **Vitamin C:** About 80 mg/day is required for the formation of collagen and also for immunity against infections and diseases. Vegetables like cabbage and lettuce taken in raw form are rich sources of vitamin C.
- ▶ **Vitamin A:** (Beta-carotene-3800 mg/day) is required for a clear vision, skin and immunity. The requirement for vitamin A increases during lactation.
- ▶ **Vitamin D:** It aids the absorption of calcium in the body and sunlight is an excellent source of vitamin D. Dietary supplements are not required.
- ▶ **Vitamin B-12:** The shortage is due to deficient vegetarian diets. *Soya milk* provides enough amount of *vitamin B-12.*
- ▶ During this period, your diet should include almonds, garlic, milk and fenugreek. These products increase and stimulate the production of breast milk.

Mostly women become bulky after the delivery of a child. How to slim the body after the delivery of the baby?

A fat surplus of *10 to 15% over the normal weight* must be taken as *overweight*. Beyond this, it is called as *obesity*. Over 30%, it is *extreme obesity*. Overweight can be of three types: *fatty overweight, watery overweight* and *cellulite.* Let us explain them.

Fatty overweight is really 'fat and muscle', hypertrophy, uniformly spread, accompanied by a large appetite and is common in men. The obesity is often noticeable over the upper half of the body, head, neck, arms and trunk.

Watery overweight is a matter of 'watery fat', which does not affect the muscles at all. The obesity is most usual over the lower half of the body, and is not accompanied by any marked appetite. It is more common in women.

Cellulite is a form of inflammation rather than overweight. Heredity factor, habit of overeating, ageing factor, poor functioning of system, nervous factor, sedentary life causing constipation and glandular system causing oversecretion by part of the sub-renal glands are some of the prominent causes of overweight.

To maintain a perfect figure and self-grooming after becoming a mother, the amount of energy you consume must be equal to the amount of energy you burn. The face becomes round and bulky. The following are certain symptoms of fatness after the childbirth:

- ▶ Shoulders get plump and hollow, and the collar-bones disappear.
- ▶ Fat overhang the hips and the waist disappears.
- ▶ The buttocks enlarge.
- ▶ The girdle shrinks and the rolls of flesh swell out above or below the girdle.
- ▶ The neck thickens and loses its normal contour. A double chin under the nape of the neck appears.
- ▶ Breasts sag down to the stomach.
- ▶ The stomach droops over the pubis and the pubis hangs over the genital organs.
- ▶ The skirt belt or jean gets a little tight and there is strain on the jacket buttons.

There are several causes of obesity, but the main are due to overeating and lack of exercise. The logic way to lose weight is to cut down the food intake by 100 per cent without affecting the nutritive value of the food consumed. Exercise regularly to burn the extra fat. *One kilogram of body fat contains 7500 calories of energy.* By having a daily calorie reduction of 500 calories, the total weight reduction in a month would be 2 kg.

The following steps are essential to reduce weight after childbirth:
- ▶ Tone up the muscles
- ▶ Improve digestion
- ▶ Increase oxygen supply to the body
- ▶ Help to keep your weight down
- ▶ Retain calcium in the body which delays the ageing process
- ▶ Keep the heart in good condition
- ▶ Help to keep a glowing skin and shining hair

Diet control:

Calories are themselves energy units and all foods contain calories to a greater or lesser amount. *A normal daily diet should contain 2000 to 2200 calories to fulfil the needs of a healthy female.* The protein intake should account for about 50% of your daily calories consumption. Carbohydrates should be kept to the minimum. *Cut down starchy foods containing sugar.*

Normally, *a healthy food can be digested within 15 to 20 minutes.* A young woman of average height, who is not pregnant or involved in hard physical labour, requires an *average 2300 calories a day.* One gram protein or carbohydrate gives four calories, whereas, one gram of fat gives nine calories. Protein is found in excess in milk, eggs, meat, fish, soybeans almonds, coconuts, groundnuts, etc to give strength to the body. Carbohydrate is found in vegetables, fruits, cereals, etc. The deficiency of carbohydrates leads to weakness. Avoid taking drastic steps in reducing weight. You are fat-prone, if you:

- ▶ Like eating
- ▶ Have rather sedentary habits or a sedentary job
- ▶ Put on weight during holidays
- ▶ Are emotionally upset and worry makes you lose weight
- ▶ Have little effect of massage and douches

Daily requirement of calories for women doing light work is 1900. A *teenager female needs daily 2200 calories.* Women doing moderate work require 2200, a pregnant woman 2500, a mother during lactation a 2900 and a belly dancer needs 3750 calories, every 24 hours.

The per hour calorie consumption required by a female is given below:
- ▶ Women engaged in light household work need 120 to 300 calories.
- ▶ Women doing hard household work need 400 to 600 calories.
- ▶ Floor sweeping women require 240 to 300 calories.
- ▶ Boating consumes 125 to 220 calories in an hour.
- ▶ Swimming consumes 395 to 475 calories per hour.
- ▶ For gardening, 200 to 250 calories are needed in an hour.

- ▶ Dancing consumes 250 to 350 calories per hour.
- ▶ For morning walk, about 150, for jogging, about 800, for cycling, 315 to 350 and for skating, 350 to 375 calories are required in an hour.

Foods you may eat after childbirth

- ▶ Non-fatty soups and slightly salted vegetables
- ▶ Eggs (one egg a day is sufficient)
- ▶ Fresh butter
- ▶ Fresh or condensed milk (skimmed and unsweetened)
- ▶ Cheese with low fat contents
- ▶ Cooked or raw green vegetables
- ▶ Fresh fruits
- ▶ Fruit juices and herbal tea

Foods you should avoid after childbirth

Types of Food that should be taken after Childbirth

- ▶ Bread, biscuits and pastries
- ▶ Mutton and fatty fish
- ▶ Fried foods, butter and oils
- ▶ Cream and milk foods
- ▶ Cornflakes, starchy flour and rice
- ▶ Fatty, fermented and salted cheese
- ▶ Banana, chestnuts, walnuts, jam, honey, cocoa and chocolates
- ▶ Wine, beer, cider, alcoholic and sweetened drinks

Important do's and don'ts

Types of Food that should be avoided after Childbirth

1. Weigh yourself every 28 hours.
2. Cut down on your food intake, especially bread, biscuits and cakes.
3. Use little salt and no sugar.
4. Have breakfast on one apple and tea.
5. Avoid drinking water, while you are eating.
6. Reduce your appetite an hour before your meals.
7. Take foam bath or if possible, take a Turkish bath.
8. Exercise for 15 to 20 minutes every morning.
9. Energetic sports may keep you slim and trim.
10. Drink diuretic water.

11. Do not lose patience.
12. Do not let yourself constipated.
13. Do not take drugs without consulting a doctor.
14. Do not weigh yourself very frequently.

How to take care of the body after childbirth?

Don't neglect your body after childbirth. Daily care can help to keep your body smooth, soft and healthy. Chin, neck, upper arms, stomach, breasts, back, waistline, hips, thighs and bottom are some of the areas of the body which require special care by every woman to maintain her personality and improve the skin texture, colour and tone.

Beauty of the neck: The neck is the most neglected area of the body. Whenever, having facial, include your neck in all facial routines, such as cleansing, toning, moisturising and nourishing. Use a special nourishing cream during night before sleep and gently massage. Massage and exercises reduce the extra fat on the neck. In winter, massage with nourishing cream or oil or cold cream mixed with a little almond oil is very beneficial.

Beauty of the Neck

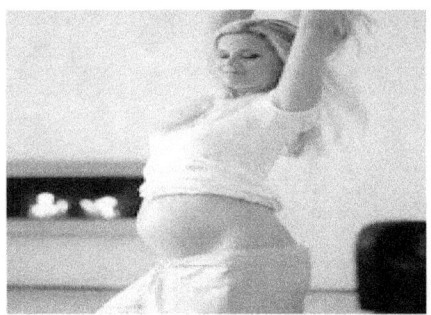
Dancing

Swimming

Rope Jumping

Walking/Jogging

Beauty of the waistline: A slim waistline makes a woman highly appealing. Waistline lends flexibility to her frame and enhance gait. Generally, the hip-bone of a woman is much broader than the man, especially after the delivery of a child. One develops a fattening tendency and the waist becomes flabby losing its natural beauty. Here are few suggestions for the attraction of waistline:

1. Massage with olive oil to prevent wrinkles, flabbiness and folds during pregnancy and after delivery on the waistline.
2. Walk, rope jumping, dancing and swimming are important exercises for the waistline.
3. Avoid the use of high pillow, it deforms and weakens the waist.
4. Use hard bed without foam mattresses.
5. Do not rely on false advertisements claiming to restore your slim waistline by the use of belts or corsets.

Hip and thigh care: Apart from having a beautiful face, if your body is disproportionate, you will lose all its charm. To have a check on your posture, arrange a mirror in such a way that you can see your side view completely. If your arms fall along the back line of your hips, then you stand with your stomach protruding. Correct your posture by holding your stomach in, so that the arms fall in the centre of the side of the body. Now if your arms fall in front, then you have probably protruding hips. Therefore, try to reduce your weight on the hips, and also bring the waist and the back a little backwards. Make efforts to push the hips forward, till your arms fall in the centre of the side of your body The body should meet the following measurements:

Bust	6 times your wrist
Waist	4 times your wrist
Hips	6-1/4 times your wrist
Thighs	3-1/2 times your wrist
Calves	2-1/4 times your wrist
Ankles	1-1/2 times your wrist

Hips and thighs are adversely affected after the delivery of the baby. *Fat hips and flabby thighs spoil the gait.* It is important to be alert immediately after the delivery, otherwise, it will be too late. It is a gradual process and hence, beauty-conscious women recognise the signals at the very beginning, and take steps to keep the body proportionate. Every woman must know the required proportions of her thighs and hips according to her height as given below:

Height (cm)	*Hips (cm)*	*Thighs (cm)*
153	85	47
155	86	49
158	87.5	51
160.5	89	52
163	91.5	53
165.5	94	56

Buttocks: The sign of sagging affects the buttocks which start sagging due to the lack of muscle tone, lack of support and elasticity in the skin. *Regular massage with anti-cellulite oils* can help break down the fatty deposits underneath the skin. There are several reducing creams available in the market to massage the buttocks, but they do not work deep down enough to work up or decrease the size of the buttocks. However, exercises specifically for the buttocks will help.

Stomach: Stretch marks on the stomach are caused due to the fibre beneath the skin surface that weakens its normal elasticity of the skin due to the weight or excess fat. These marks mostly occur after the childbirth and sometimes appear in puberty when the growth rate of the body is fast. Apply olive or baby oil throughout pregnancy and immediately after childbirth. Lubricating the skin as a part of daily routine helps to minimise these stretch marks. The marks may also fade a little with regular application of a cream containing a large concentration of Vitamin E. More serious stretch marks require surgery. Exercises stimulating stomach muscles will help.

Breast beauty: If you have mottled-looking skin on the breasts, stimulate circulation with alternative rinse of hot and cold water. This will help to minimise the problem and make your bosom firmer. If the skin looks wrinkled and sagging, particularly when you are feeding a baby, use a good moisturising cream. Breasts require maximum attention after delivery. Breasts usually sag, if the infant is suckled while sitting in a faulty posture. Suckling with the infant in both lap or suckling in the lying down position are harmful for the breasts. Do not forget to press the nipples immediately after breastfeeding and remove the remaining milk with a couple of jerks. This gives lightness and freshness to the breasts.

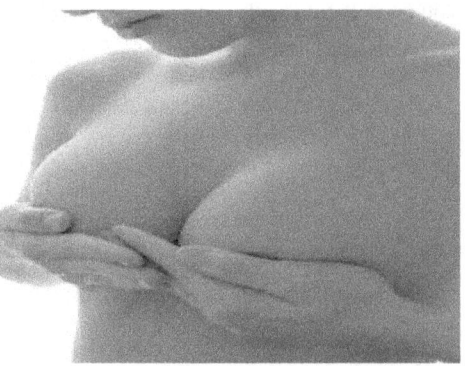
Breast Beauty

Back: Spotty back are often a problem for people who tend to have a greasy or combination of greasy facial skin. The overactive sebaceous glands that cause the secretions which start the spots are themselves stimulated by hormonal activity in the body, particularly during adolescence. The only remedy is to keep the skin scrupulously clean by washing with a medicated liquid soap daily and by changing the clothes. To avoid unnecessary irritation, choose cotton for the vest, bra, blouse or T-shirt. Apply medicated cleansing lotion and anti-acne cream to dry up the excess grease at bed-time. If a spot appears on the back, just before you plan to wear a low-backed or backless dress, disguise it with a medicated make-up matching your skin tone. Here are a few tips for the beauty of the back:

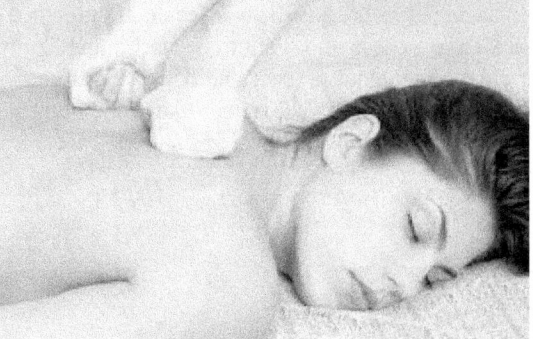
Back Massage

1. As far as possible, use medicated soap to heal rashes.
2. Massage you back with mustard oil before taking bath.
3. Rub anti-acne lotion at night.
4. Wear loose dresses to avoid itching.
5. Rubbing lemon on the skin of the back clears one's skin of its dark patches usually appearing during pregnancy. Rubbing lemon is also effective for a dark complexioned skin. Cut a lemon in two pieces, rub on the back, and let the juice dry for ten minutes followed by washing off with cold water.
6. If you have unwanted hair on the back, this can be hidden by bleaching. Use a face pack on the back, which ensures a beautiful, soft, lustrous skin. Mix to it few drops of hydrogen peroxide and mustard oil in the pack.

Bottom: Bottoms are sun and air starved, and even in summer, these are covered, so tend to look pale and pasty. Nude sunbathing is impractical for Indian women but instead of that you can use ultraviolet lamp for few seconds every day. Your bottom is also adversely affected during pregnancy and during labour-pains. Use plenty of body lotion and moisturiser on this area. Pinching the flesh on the bottom when you are in a bathing tub is good for circulation and shape and reduces extra flesh.

What are the necessary steps to get rid of the flab after childbirth?

Mindset: The success of your weight reduction fairly depends on your will power, keenness and attitude - without which nothing really works.

Right aim: Looking to lose immediately is an unrealistic and unreasonable goal. Aim to reduce weight gradually, not quickly.

Exercising: Make exercise an integral part of your daily routine. Brisk walking, cycling, playing tennis or badminton, swimming, aerobics and yoga are some of the easy exercises, Start up with a 10-minute routine and gradually increase it to 30-40 minutes daily.

Change in lifestyle: Lifestyle changes are must. If you are having sedentary habits, you are likely to lose more than gain. Avoid making obesity, a way of life. Walk briskly, taking to the stairs instead of riding the lift or an elevator are good habits.

Diet control: Exercise control over your diet to lose weight. Remember, *crash dieting* is *unhealthy*, though it works well initially but leaves worse effects. You put on whatever weight you had lost. Eat slowly, avoid going to a party on an empty stomach, Eating a low or no-fat diet and consuming more of fibre-rich and unrefined foods are some of the good habits.

Don't skip meals: Skipping a meal and ending up eating more at the next meal is rather harmful.

Avoid late dinner: Watch what you eat after 7 pm, as the food you eat late is stored in the body as *pure lard*. Food enters the *blood stream as energy after four hours of taking dinner.* Since the body does not need energy, so the food is stored in the fat cells as fat. As far as possible, have light dinner.

Release toxins: Water helps washing away the toxins from the body. Start the day with a glass of water.

Skip meal: If you feel hungry in the evening, snack up but skip dinner. If you had a heavy lunch, then just take a bowl of soup for dinner.

Maintain food diary: In spite of diet control, if you have not reduced at all, although visiting a gym or a health club regularly, then maintain a food diary. Make a record of everything you eat or drink from the time you wake up early in the morning till night as you go to bed for two weeks. You will find your wrongs.

What are the necessary care after a baby's birth?

After a baby's birth, a mother feels exhausted, fatigued and let down and her body undergoes rapid physical and hormonal changes. For early recovery, very frequently check your temperature, pulse, respiratory rate, blood pressure and monitor the amount and character of *lochia* (red-coloured, fleshy-odour discharge from the vagina flowing heavily for the first day after the birth of the baby, which diminishes in a week's time changing its colour to pale pink in next 3 to 4 days and finally becomes yellowish white or brown with the presence of bloody clots for 6 to 8 weeks). Avoid infection or overexertion, which cause excessive bleeding. In such case consult your doctor.

There are few more problems faced by the mother during the postpartum period, as below:

- **After-pains:** Painful contractions of the uterus occur. To cope with the pain, relax and use the slow-breathing patterns. After pains may disappear after a week.
- **Cervix conditioning:** The cervix shrinks to its pre-pregnant size but remains somewhat wider for few months.
- **Vaginal toning:** The vagina gradually regains its tone, but the labia remain looser, larger and darker as compared to the pre-pregnancy condition.
- **Breasts:** Breasts secrete *colostrums* (a yellow fluid that precedes breast milk). The milk production starts between the 2nd and 5th day after the delivery. During this period, the breasts may feel tense, hard to the touch and painful (engorged). Non-breastfeeding mothers still produce milk. To suppress lactation, breast binding, ice packs and avoidance of breast stimulation help diminish milk production. Do not express milk from the breasts, as this will stimulate the breasts to produce more milk.
- **Circulatory changes:** Some blood loss is natural after childbirth. Average blood loss amounts to approximate one cup in normal delivery, but may be double in case of an *episiotomy* (vaginal cut at the time of delivery). Slight blood lost during the childbirth is not harmful, but if blood losses are more, consult a doctor.
- **Stretch marks and pigmentation of the abdominal skin:** After the birth, the abdominal muscles remain soft for about six weeks and stretch marks appear. These marks fade with the passage of time but do not disappear completely. However, skin pigmentation will fade away after few months.
- **Hormonal changes:** After childbirth, the body undergoes sudden and dramatic changes in hormonal production. The hormone producing level drops abruptly and remains low until the ovaries begin producing these hormones again. If a woman breast-feed, she may not menstruate for several months, though ovulation can occur during this time. However, if a mother is not breastfeeding, she will begin menstruating within 4 to 6 weeks after the birth. First few menstrual periods following delivery may be heavier than usual, but will return to normal soon.

- ▶ **Rest and activities:** Adequate rest is essential to recover after childbirth. Try to rest an extra two hours daily and go to bed early at night.
- ▶ **Exercise:** Perform the pelvic floor contraction exercise (known as *Kegel*) to heal episiotomy or any tear, reduce the swelling and restore the muscle tone in the pelvic floor. Try to begin post-partum exercises within a day or two in case of a normal delivery. Better consult your doctor in this regard. The conditioning exercises during pregnancy help you recover former contours and strength during the post-partum period. Two areas of the body: abdominal muscles and pelvic floor muscles (to reduce swelling, increase circulation and promote healing in the perineum and restore the vaginal muscle tone) need special attention.
- ▶ **Uterus examination:** Fundus can be felt midway between the navel and the pubic bone. Massage the uterus, which helps to maintain the firmness of the uterus, prevent heavy blood loss from the placental site and return to its previous size. By the end of 5 to 6 weeks, the uterus returns to its previous size.
- ▶ **Sexual adjustments:** Some men and women want to resume sexual intercourse as soon as possible after the birth, though most of the females feel constrained or afraid and lack enjoying making love due to a sore perineum and extreme fatigue. If you are not ready to resume intercourse early, you may resume pleasuring (touching and enjoying each other's bodies sensually with or without orgasm). It is suggested to refrain from intercourse for at least six weeks after the birth. It is, however, safe to have intercourse when stitches heal, vaginal discharge stops and you feel you like it. There is decrease in vaginal lubrication after childbirth because of hormonal changes. The problem can be alleviated by use of a sterile, water soluble lubricant, such as K-Y jelly or contraceptive cream during intercourse. Remember, conception can occur whether or not menstruation has resumed. The condom along with spermicidal foam, cream or jelly is safe and is an effective method after childbirth.
- ▶ **Don't skip meals:** Skipping a meal and ending up eating more at the next meal is rather harmful.
- ▶ **Avoid late dinner:** Watch what you eat after 7 pm, as the food you eat late is stored in the body as pure *lard*. Food enters the bloodstream as *energy* after four hours of taking dinner. Since the body does not need energy, so the food is stored in the fat cells as fat. As far as possible, have light dinner.

Chapter 7

Breast & Breastfeeding

𝓑reastfeeding is one of the most exciting, memorable and enjoyable experience for a woman. But, unfortunately there are many women who have not kept up with the news research finding about the nutritional and immunological advantages of human milk for infants. In the recent years, there has been explosion of research into the properties and benefits of breast milk, the value of nursing for both mother and infant and also the practices enhancing or hinder the course of breastfeeding. According to medical experts and researches, there is nothing as good as breast milk for the newborn.

In this chapter, attempt has been made to provide the expert's advice on everything a mother ought to know to make nursing rewarding. What is exactly required of nursing is the skill of easy breastfeeding. Efforts has been made to describe the details in the basics of

Breastfeeding

nursing like proper positioning of the baby for nursing, enhancing milk supply, expressing milk by hand or a breast pump, successful breastfeeding, diets and nutrition for feeding mothers, exercises and massage to keep the breasts fit, need to be taken care of during pregnancy and nursing and above all, it acquaints with the common breast disorders and diseases including *mammography* by a skilful blend of professional experience.

Engorgement of the breasts, block ducts and mastitis, sore nipples, breast cancer, leakage of milk from the breast during pregnancy period (nipple discharge), etc, are some of the common breast disorders detailed in this chapter with an advice to treat them by expert gynaecologists.

Surgical Delivery

If the foetal head is stuck higher up, *a cesarean delivery is needed and surgery is required.* A cesarean section should not be the last resort of the obstetrician after other methods of delivery have been attempted and have failed. Now the cesarean birth is a relatively safe, surgical operation in which the baby is born through the incision in the uterine and abdominal walls instead of through the vagina. An incision is made horizontally at the lower part of the abdomen, the baby and the placenta are removed through a cut in uterus and abdomen and closed by stitching. In an emergency delivery, the baby is removed out by a long vertical cut.

A cesarean birth may be indicated for the following reasons:

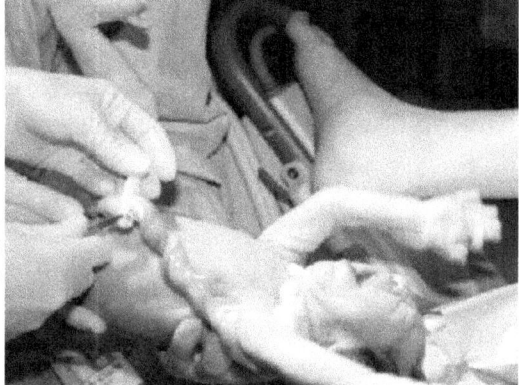
Surgical Delivery

- ▶ When there is a space problem for a large baby or a small pelvic structure or a combination of the two.
- ▶ When the baby is situated unfavourably for a vaginal birth.
- ▶ When the contractions are poor or the dilation and descent are not progressing.
- ▶ Due to changes in the foetal heart rate when the baby's oxygen supply has been reduced.
- ▶ When the umbilical cord descends through the vagina before the baby is delivered resulting in a reduced oxygen supply.
- ▶ When the placenta covers the cervix.
- ▶ When the placenta prematurely separates from the uterine wall.
- ▶ When the expectant mother has toxemia, diabetes, high blood pressure, heart disease or other conditions, when she or the baby in the womb may not be able to withstand the stress of labour and vaginal birth.
- ▶ In case of repeated cesarean, where there may be risk of uterine rupture.
- ▶ Avoid cesarean section in cases of a cardiac patient.

Common symptoms just before the delivery

Every expecting mother should be familiar with the symptoms as the time of delivery arrives nearer. At this time, a woman requires lots of love, affection and confidence from her husband and other family members to overcome the pain and discomfort.

The following symptoms are observed just before a delivery:

- ▶ The sudden onset of labour pains is brought on.
- ▶ There is an urge for frequent urination.
- ▶ The low position of the foetal head makes walking and sitting difficult.
- ▶ There is backache and tiredness in the limbs.
- ▶ Vaginal secretion increases; as it may be blood stained. Tightness in the abdomen area due to uterine contractions.

Why should a child breastfeed?

If we look at the past, in the early 1900, mostly the babies were breastfed or fed by the cow's milk. Solid foods were not offered till the age of one year. In 1920, people started offering solid foods. By 1975, a change had taken place, but still breast milk was more popular. Today, over 60% mothers breastfeed.

Breast milk is recommended for many reasons:
- ▶ It is an ideal food for the newly born babies.
- ▶ It is easily digested.
- ▶ Contains antibodies that protect the baby from infections.
- ▶ Reduces the possibility of allergic reactions.
- ▶ Aids involution and returns the uterus to its normal size.
- ▶ Makes special intimate relations between the mother and the baby.
- ▶ Is convenient and economical.

In some cases as below, breastfeeding is not recommended:
- ▶ If the mother has had extensive breast reduction surgery.
- ▶ The mother has hepatitis.
- ▶ Mother's breasts are infected with beta streptococcus or active herpes.
- ▶ The mother is taking drugs for cancer, seizure preventing drugs and radioactive materials.

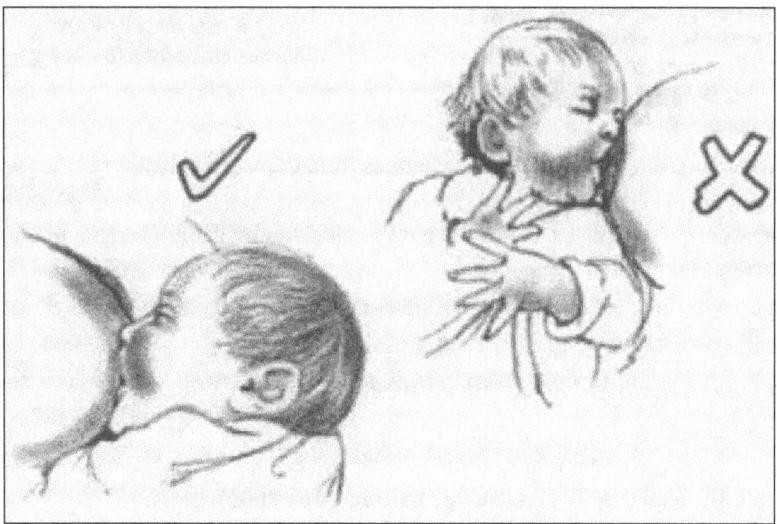

Correct or Incorrect Way of Breastfeeding

How to take care of the breasts during pregnancy?

Ensure to make a right choice for wearing bra during pregnancy, as below:
- ▶ The bra should be made of cotton and not of synthetic material.
- ▶ The bra should be well fitting o support the extra weight of the breasts during pregnancy and at the time of lactation.
- ▶ The bra should not be too tight as to compress the breasts as the pressure on the breasts can harm the glands besides causing pain and irritation.
- ▶ Remove bra during night. An ideal dress a pregnant woman should wear during night is a loose gown.

- ▶ Avoid washing nipples with soap or wipe away the greasy material as this may result in soreness of the nipples. Just splash plain water to keep nipples clean.

How to take care of breasts during lactation?

Breasts are considered an important part of a woman's sex appeal. It is important to understand what is likely to happen to the breasts for the woman breastfeeding her baby. The breasts enlarge because of the milk and the nipples enlarge and darken. The shape of the breasts can be preserved if a woman takes care of and wears well-fitting brassiere to support the breasts. The shape of the breasts usually changes with age.

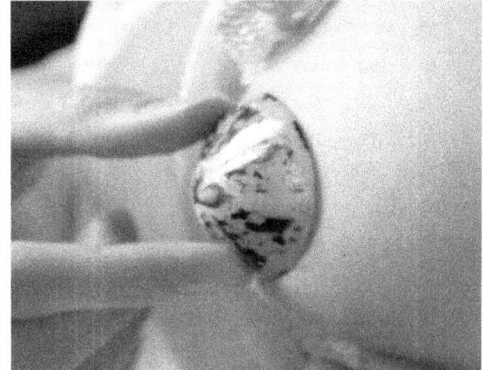
Care of Breast during Lactation

Following care should be taken for the breasts during lactation:

- ▶ Keep the breasts and nipples clean and try to prevent them from becoming sore and infected.
- ▶ Do not use soap to clean the nipples and the areola; it will make them sore.
- ▶ Do not let the nipples remain moist for long; this will lead to cracking and infection.
- ▶ Keep a clean piece of cloth or a pad in your bra cup when breastfeeding to absorb leakage of milk. Make sure to change the cloth after feeding.
- ▶ Often breast nipples secrete oil. There is no need to clean the secretions from the nipples, since these protect the nipples from infection.
- ▶ If the nipples are not soft and supple, apply some cream or oil. Avoid using mustard oil as it irritates the sensitive skin. Wash the cream or oil before breastfeeding.
- ▶ Expose the nipples and the breasts to air daily for some time.
- ▶ Prevent engorgement of breasts by emptying them immediately after breastfeeding.
- ▶ Make sure to empty the breasts after breastfeeding to relieve tension. Press the areola so that the milk comes out and removes the remaining milk with a couple of jerks.
- ▶ Do not feed the child when sleeping in incorrect posture; this may cause *breast sagging*. Always let the baby suckle in a sitting position with the child in the lap and your hand supporting the head.
- ▶ Wash the breasts with hot and cold baths simultaneously for 4 to 5 times daily to ensure proper blood circulation.
- ▶ Wear well-fitting bra, while exercising. Not wearing bra when exercising further spoil the shape of the bust-line. Swimming is an ideal exercise to improve the shape of the breasts.
- ▶ Nurse the baby soon after the birth. This will help enhance the flow of milk and the engorgement is less of a problem.
- ▶ Get into a comfortable position. Sit comfortably supported or lie on your side. If your perineum is sore, ask for an ice bag to ease the pain and help you relaxed while breastfeeding.

- If you have had a cesarean, sitting in the bed with the baby across your lap on a pillow may be comfortable.
- Nurse your newborn in a calm atmosphere, which allow you and your baby to concentrate on feeding.
- Now grasp your breast with your free hand behind the areola and compress the nipple with the thumb and forefinger aligning the nipple with the baby's mouth.
- Stroke your baby's cheek with your nipple. Bring your baby to your breast rather than bringing your breast to your baby.
- Let your baby suckle at each breast for at least 10 minutes.
- Make sure as much of your areola as possible is in the baby's mouth to ensure a good latch.
- Arouse your baby's sense of taste by expressing a few drops of colostrums and rubbing nipples on the baby's lips.
- Breastfeed on demand – every one to three hours or 10 to 15 times a day to establish an adequate milk supply.

I have very heavy breasts. Suggest

There are no muscles in the breasts and they consist mainly of the mammary glands and fat. Mammoplasty is a modern cosmetic surgery, in which breast reduction is performed to the desired size in case of overdeveloped breasts by reducing the excess breast tissue and lifting the

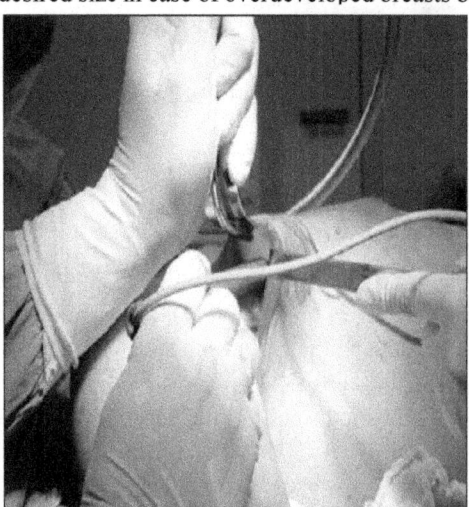
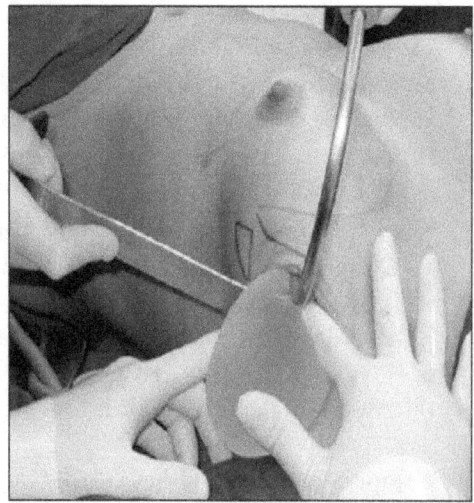

A   B
Mammoplasty

gland if the breast sags. Some people fear that breast reduction increases the chances of breast cancer but studies have given no evidence of it. The main cause of overdevelopment of breasts is *hyperactivity of the female hormones during puberty*. Sometimes, the breasts may grow to pathologically abnormal size. During pregnancy, the breasts may become enlarged but regain their original shape and size after childbirth. Obese women generally have overdeveloped breast, which is known as 'fatty macromastia'.

Breast & Breastfeeding

Women with abnormally enlarged breasts feel the following symptoms:
- ▶ Strain on cervical and thoracic vertebrae resulting in pain in the neck and backache.
- ▶ The brassiere may become a painful embodiment during menstrual period.
- ▶ Sagging breasts create problems between the lower part of the breasts and the chest wall.
- ▶ Pressure on the neck or nerve plexus due to the weight of the heavy breasts.

Breast cancer is a malignant condition caused by the abnormal rapid multiplication of cells in a part of body in women more common in *cervix, uterus or breasts*. According to a medical survey, out of the total numbers of cancers reported, *over 40% are cervical cancers, 12% breast cancers*, nearly *10% uterus cancers*, about *10% throat cancers* and rest nearly 30%. The usual age to be afflicted by cancer is between 30 and 50.

Breast self-examination:

The following steps are undertaken:
- ▶ Examine the breasts standing before a mirror for symmetry in size and shape and retraction of the nipples.
- ▶ Raise your arms over the head and study the breasts for similar signs.
- ▶ Recline on bed with a pillow under the shoulder on the side of the breast to be examined.
- ▶ Raise your arms over the head to examine the inner half of the breast. Begin at the breastbone and palpate the inner half of the breast.
- ▶ Carefully palpate the area over the nipples with flats of fingers.
- ▶ Now examine the lower half of the breasts.
- ▶ With arm down the side, examine the breast by carefully feeling the tissues extending to the armpit.
- ▶ Examine the upper outer part of the breast with the flat part of the fingers.
- ▶ Finally, examine the lower outer part of the breast with the flat of the fingers in successive stages.

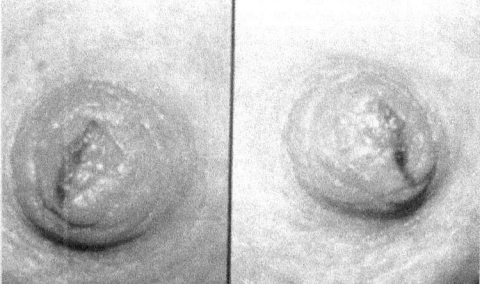
Cracked Sore Nipples

If there is only a single nodule or lump in the breast, this is more likely to be malignant, if there is no pain. The tissue is removed by surgical procedure. In case of symptoms of cancer, immediate treatment is required. If the cancer appears to have spread to the neighbouring lymph nodes, the patient should be given extensive radiation therapy to the whole affected area. Self-examination of breasts should be conducted once a month.

When the cancer is present in the breast, the following symptoms are observed:
- ▶ There is usually one hard single lump with no pain.
- ▶ There may be a slight blood discharge from the nipple. Although the disease may occur at any time of life, it is much more common between the age of 35 and 60. After the *age of 65, breast cancer is rare*.
- ▶ Painful breasts.

- Formation of painful abscess.
- Excessive watery discharge from the nipples.

What are the common breastfeeding problems?

- **Difficulty with let down reflex**: Anxiety, fatigue, inadequate nipple stimulation, taking excessive amount of alcohol, caffeine and smoking, especially during the hour before feeding, may inhibit the let down reflex.
- **Reduced milk supply**: Fatigue, insufficient intake of fluids and calories or poor diet may reduce milk supply.
- **Poor latch**: If the baby has not positioned his mouth properly on the nipple, he will be unable to compress the areola properly, and will not stimulate a let down reflex. This may lead to the baby making a clicking sound during sucking.
- **Engorgement:** There are two causes – increased blood supply and accumulation, of milk in the breasts.

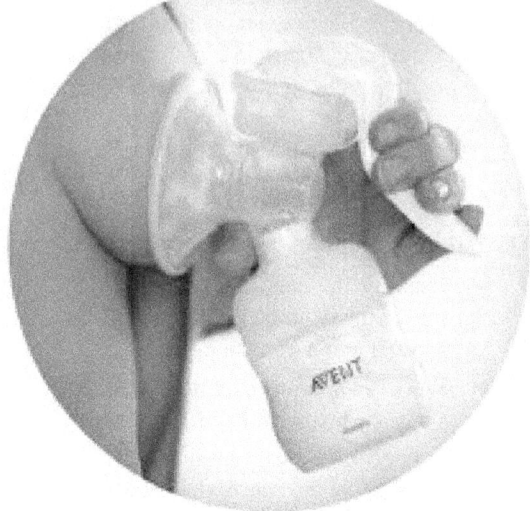

Breast Pump

In such cases symptoms like swelling and hardness in the breasts. In such cases the suggested treatments include wearing a well-fitting bra during day and night for support to the breasts. Make sure that no area of the breast is compressed. Apply cold pack to reduce blood flow to the breasts. Express milk while standing in a warm shower. Cover the breasts with warm, loist towel. Express milk before feeding to soften a hard, swollen areola. Remember, breast massage stimulates the milk flow. Use an electric or mechanical breast pump to relieve the fullness in the breasts.

- **Flat and inverted nipples**: *Poor shape of nipples interferes with feeding.* If the nipples appear flat or inverted, it is advised to press the areola between the thumb and the finger to help the nipple to stick out and thus, the baby will not have any difficulty in suckling. Do not apply cream or ointment on your nipples nor, it is necessary to wash them with soap.
- **Cracked and sore nipples:** This condition occurs usually in the first week of nursing due to improper positioning of the baby's mouth on the areola or the poor latch. There is

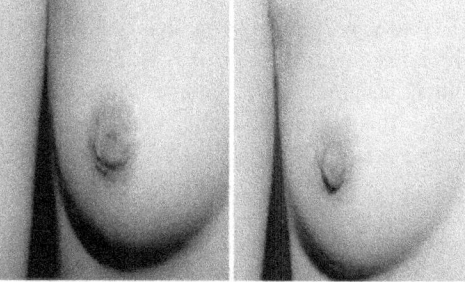

Flat and Inverted Nipples

difference between a crack and a fissure. A fissure is generally at the base of nipple and more painful, and sometimes the blood may ooze out of it. In case of a crack, a mother doesn't have to take the baby of breastfeed. To prevent crack or sore nipples, wash your breasts with plain water and keep them dry in between the feeds as *wet nipples tend to become sore*. Do not apply soap on the nipples. Make sure that the baby's mouth is correctly positioned on your nipple. Feed the baby more frequently and start feeding on the less sore nipples. Apply oil or cream to keep nipples soft and supple. Do not apply mustard oil. Clean nipples after feeding.

▶ Expose the nipples and breast to air (sunshine or sun lamp) for some time daily. Apply oil or cream during pregnancy. At this time, a greasy material is usually produced, which keeps the nipples supple. In case of leakage of milk, use a piece of clean cloth to absorb it. Keep the cloth in cups of your bra. Always wear a clean bra. Change the feeding position very frequently. Try sitting, lying or using a football hold so that the pressure from the baby's sucking will not be in the same place all the time. Dry the nipple air dry with your bra flaps or set a hair dryer. Apply an ice pack to the sore area before feeding at the breast. Express a small amount of breast milk and rub it over the sore area. Breast milk has the healing properties. Use a nipple shield readily available in the market in case of a severe problem.

▶ **Blockage of milk in the breast:** The main reason for this disorder is milk of thick density unable to secrete through the blocked tube. It starts accumulating behind the blocked tube resulting in pain. Feeding mothers may also have symptoms of fever in such condition. At times, tubes get blocked because of wearing tight bras. Always wear bras, which do not exert pressure on the breasts. T is suggested that mothers suffering from this disorder should continue to breastfeed from the affected breast first so that the milk instead of accumulating and aggravating the problem drains, thus relieving the block. Massage the affected breast towards the nipple. After feeding the nipple express the breasts. You may consult a doctor if you are not getting relief.

▶ The pain and tension can be relieved by hot and cold compresses. If proper care is not taken, there are chances of mastitis suffering. In case of engorged nipple, the flow of milk in the tubes gets blocked and milk starts leaking into the infected part of the breast. In case of mastitis, the infected part of the breast becomes red, painful, swollen and shiny because of stretching of the skin. However, you may continue feeding the child, because in spite of infection the germs do not pass into the milk and the baby will not suffer. A mother suffering from mastitis may develop an abscess if she discontinues breastfeeding

▶ **Epidemic Mastitis:** Swelling of breasts with severe pain, a tender, reddened, hot breast, nausea, fatigue are some of the symptoms of epidemic mastitis and you should consult a doctor for the treatment and find out whether to feed the baby or not. Drainage of milk is the only remedy for getting relief from the pain. Sometimes, pus may also ooze along with the milk. The patient may also have fever. To unclog, the ducts apply warm moist pack or a warm towel to the affected area. Massage the area towards the nipple. Perform wide circle exercise for quick relief. To do this exercise, rotate both

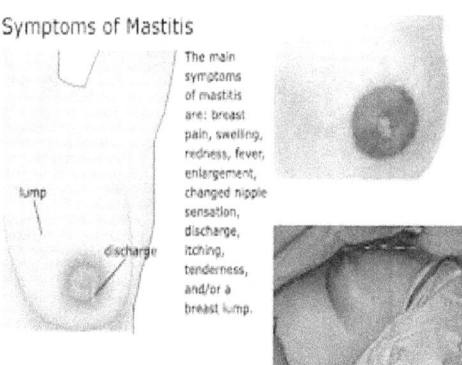

Epidemic Mastitis

arms five to eight times in circles without wearing a bra to strengthen the nerves and unclog the ducts. If you have an abscess in one of the breasts, you should continue feeding the baby with the other breast. Express milk. Make sure the mastitis breast is as empty as possible after feeding. Take antibiotics as prescribed by the doctor only. Drink lots of water, juice and other fluids. Rest and stay in the bed as much as possible. There are many ways to express milk by hand or a breast pump. Express by hand conveniently.

▶ Once the breast is flowing, grasp your breast at the back of the areola and press towards your chest. As you compress the areola, milk may drip or spurt into a collecting bottle. Breast pump is an effective equipment designed to squeeze out milk. Never wear anything tight or uncomfortable during pregnancy. Avoid tight bands around the waist.

Chapter-8

AIDS

AIDS stands for *Acquired Immune Deficiency Syndrome*. *Acquired* means you can get infected with it; *Immune Deficiency* means a weakness in the body's system that fights diseases. *Syndrome* means a group of health problems that make up a disease.

AIDS is caused by a virus called *HIV*, (*Human Immunodeficiency Virus*). If one gets infected with HIV, the body tries to fight the infection. It will make "antibodies", special molecules that are supposed to fight HIV. When one gets a blood test for HIV, the test looks for these antibodies. If one has them in their blood, it means that he has HIV infection. People who have the HIV antibodies are called HIV-Positive.

Being HIV-positive, or having HIV disease, is not the same as having AIDS. Many people are HIV-positive but don't get sick for many years. As HIV disease continues, it slowly wears down the immune system. Viruses, parasites, fungi and bacteria that usually don't cause any problems can make you very sick if your immune system is damaged. These are called opportunistic infections.

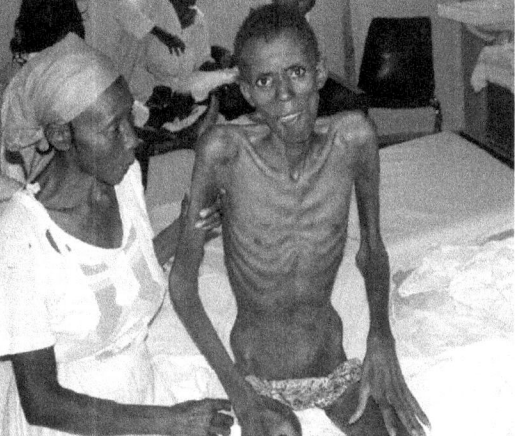

AIDS Patient

How does one get AIDS?
One doesn't actually get AIDS. He might get infected with HIV, and later might develop AIDS.

One can get infected with HIV from anyone who's infected, even if they don't look sick, and even if they haven't tested HIV-positive yet. The blood, vaginal fluid, semen and breast milk of people infected with HIV has enough of the virus in it to infect other people. Most people get the HIV virus by:

- ▶ Having sex with an infected person.
- ▶ Sharing a needle (shooting drugs) with someone who's infected
- ▶ Being born when the mother is infected, or drinking the breastmilk of an infected woman.
- ▶ Getting a transfusion of infected blood used to be a way people got AIDS, but now the blood supply is screened very carefully and the risk is extremely low.

There are no documented cases of HIV being transmitted by tears or saliva, but it is possible to be infected with HIV through oral sex or in rare cases through deep kissing, especially if you have open sores in your mouth or bleeding gums.

In India, there are a large number of people who are HIV-positive and majority of people are living with AIDS. Each year, new infections are added to cause death. However, newer treatments have cut the AIDS death rate significantly.

What happens if one is HIV Positive?

You might not know if one gets infection by HIV may get fever, headache, sore muscles and joints, stomach ache, swollen lymph glands, or a skin rash for one or two weeks. Most people think it's the flu. Some people have no symptoms. The virus will multiply in the body for a few weeks or even months before the immune system responds. During this time, one won't test positive for HIV, but can infect other people. When immune system of affected person responds, it starts to make antibodies. When this happens, one will test positive for HIV.

After the first flu-like symptoms, some people with HIV stay healthy for ten years or longer. But during this time, HIV is damaging the immune system. Without treatment, one might start having signs of HIV disease like fevers, night sweats, diarrhoea, or swollen lymph nodes. If one has HIV disease, these problems will last more than a few days, and probably continue for several weeks.

How does one know if a person has AIDS?

HIV disease becomes AIDS when immune system is seriously damaged. If one gets an opportunistic infection, he has AIDS. There is an 'official' list of opportunistic infections, put out by the Centers for Disease Control (CDC). The most common ones are:

- ▶ PCP (Pneumocystis carinii pneumonia), a lung infection;
- ▶ KS (Kaposi's sarcoma), a skin cancer;
- ▶ CMV (Cytomegalovirus), an infection that usually affects the eyes; and
- ▶ Candida, a fungal infection that can cause thrush (a white film in your mouth) or infections in your throat or vagina.
- ▶ AIDS-related diseases also includes serious weight loss, brain tumours, and other health problems. Without treatment, these opportunistic infections can kill you.

AIDS is different in every infected person. Some people die soon after getting infected, while others live fairly normal lives for many years, even after they "officially" have AIDS. A few HIV-positive people stay healthy for many years even without taking anti-HIV medications.

Is there any cure for AIDS?

There is no cure for AIDS. However, there are drugs that can slow down the HIV virus, and slow down the damage to the immune system. But there is no way to get all the HIV out of body. There are other drugs that you can take to prevent or to treat the *Opportunistic Infections (OIs)*. In most cases, these drugs work very well. The newer, stronger anti-HIV drugs have also helped reduce the rates of most OIs. A few OIs, however, are still very difficult to treat and till to date, it is a fatal disease.

What precautions/preventive measures one must take to avoid or prevent this dreaded disease?

- ▶ **Getting Sexually Transmitted:** Despite considerable investment and research, there is currently no HIV and AIDS vaccine, and microbicides (designed to prevent HIV being passed on during sex) are still undergoing trials. However, there are other ways that people can protect themselves from HIV infection, which are the basis of HIV prevention efforts around the world.

▶ **Education about HIV** and how it is spread is an essential part of HIV prevention. HIV education needs to be culturally appropriate and can take place in various settings, for example, *lessons at school, media campaigns, or peer education*. If a person has sexual intercourse with someone who has HIV, they can become infected. **'Safer sex'** refers to things that a person can do to minimise their risk of HIV infection during sexual intercourse; most importantly, using condoms consistently and correctly.

A person can be certain that they are protected against HIV infection by choosing not to have sex at all, or by only doing things that do not involve any blood or sexual fluid from one person getting into another person's body. This kind of sexual activity is the only thing that can be considered 'safe sex'.

▶ **Effective sex education** is important for providing young people with the Knowledge and Skills to protect themselves from sexual transmission of HIV.

▶ **Preventing transmission of HIV through blood:** A person can protect himself or herself against HIV infection by ensuring that HIV infected blood does not enter his or her body.

Injecting drug users who share injecting equipment or works are at risk of HIV infection. Needle exchange programmes can help to prevent HIV transmission among drug users by providing clean needles and disposing of used ones.

Healthcare workers can be exposed to HIV infected blood while at work. The most effective way to limit their risk of HIV infection is to use universal precautions with every patient, for example washing hands and wearing protective barriers (gloves, aprons, goggles, etc.) In the event that a healthcare worker is exposed to potentially HIV infected blood at work, PEP (Post Exposure Prophylaxis) is recommended as an HIV prevention measure.

▶ **Preventing mother to child transmission of HIV**

Mother-to-child transmission of HIV can be prevented by using antiretroviral drugs, which reduce the chances of a child becoming infected with HIV from around 25% to less than 2%. Once a child is born, safer infant feeding practices can also greatly reduce the risk of HIV being passed on from the mother to the child.

For these precautions to be taken, an HIV positive mother must firstly be aware of her status. This is why HIV testing in pregnancy is a crucial prevention measure.

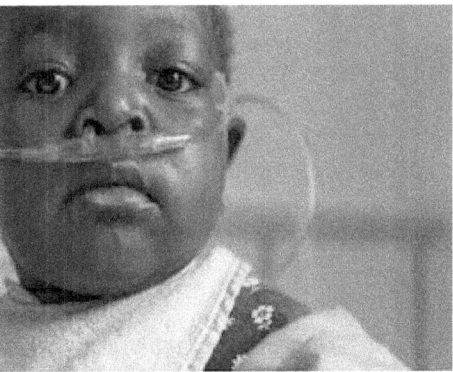

Child Transmission of HIV

Chapter-9

Vaginal Diseases

Venereal Diseases

Venereal diseases or sexually transmitted diseases (STD) can complicate and endanger pregnancy. If you have or have had an STD, you must tell your doctor, because your expected baby risks disease, death or both. In past, common infections associated with the intercourse were syphilis and gonorrhea. Today other highly contagious infections including genital herpes and few others described in this chapter have developed causing serious problems for the baby.

If an expectant mother or her partner has or has had sores, discharge from the vagina, difficulties with urination or other genital discomforts, tell your doctor so that you can be tested and possibly treated, which may be antibiotics or other treatments. Cesarean birth is the treatment of choice if one has herpes or sores in or around the vagina when labour begins, since the baby can become seriously infected while passing through the vagina.

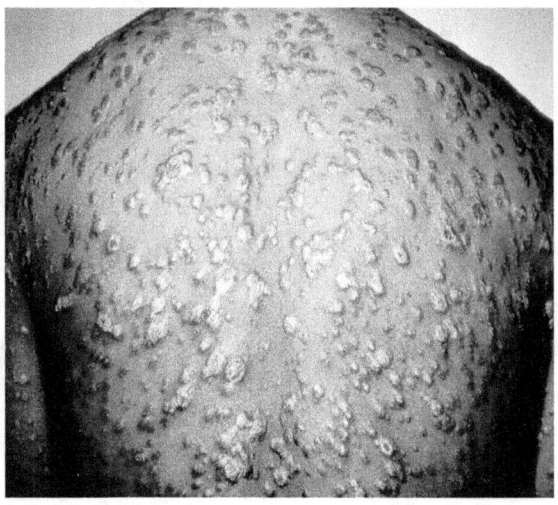

Venereal Diseases

What are the common warning signs during pregnancy?

Inform your doctors in case of the following warning signs:

Vaginal bleeding: It may lead to miscarriage, Placenta previa, Placenta disorders or a premature labour.

Abdominal pain: It may be a case of ectopic pregnancy, abruptio placenta or early labour contractions.

Leaking of fluid from vagina: Rupture of the membranes.

Puffiness or swelling of hands, feet, face: Pre-eclampsia (toxemia).

Vaginal Diseases

Severe, persistent headache: Pre-eclampsia (toxemia).

Vision disturbance, blind spots and flashes: Pre-eclampsia (toxemia).

Dizziness, light headedness, hypo tension: Pre-eclampsia or supine hypotension.

Pain or burning on urination: Urinary tract infection or a sexually transmitted disease.

Irritating vaginal discharge, sores, itching: Vaginal infection and STD.

Persistent nausea or vomiting: Hyperemesis gravidarum or an infection.

What are some of the common venereal diseases and their remedies?

Every male or female should have a thorough knowledge of venereal diseases, which prove fatal if not cared timely. Here are a few fatal venereal diseases:

Syphilis

A dangerous venereal disease caused by a small corkscrew-shaped tiny germ transmitted from male to female and vice versa through sexual contact. In few cases syphilis is acquired through contaminated material and even through injections or blood transfusions, if the germs are present in the blood. If a mother is infected with syphilis, the germs may find their way into the child's' body before birth.

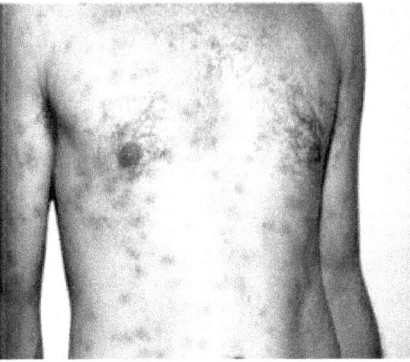

Syphilis

Prominent signs and symptoms of disease in males is a painless sore on the penis lasting several weeks and in females there may be sore deep in the vagina. Initially, the germs are confined to these areas, and later they are carried to all parts of the body through the blood and spread. Tumours or swellings may appear on various parts of the body causing severe inflammation and degeneration, which lead to headache, loss of memory, tremors of the lips, tongue, fingers, hands, change in the pupils of the eyes, loss of vision, vomiting, abdominal pain and developing large ulcers on the toes, heels and soles. Pregnant women suffering from syphilis may pass on the disease to their unborn child in growing foetus resulting in serious conditions. Soon after the birth the bones of the child sometimes appear deformed, the liver and spleen enlarged, damage to the brain and central nervous system causing the birth of a mentally and physically retarded child. A syphilitic pregnant expectant mother runs the risk of recurrent abortions and stillbirths due to the infection, damage to placenta and the growing embryo.

Here is a natural remedy to treat syphilis:

Ground in water a tablespoon of Hirankhuri booti (corchorus fascicularis) and few grains of pepper. Strain and take for two to three weeks. The patient should take a salt-free diet and avoid taking bitter, sour and pungent substances.

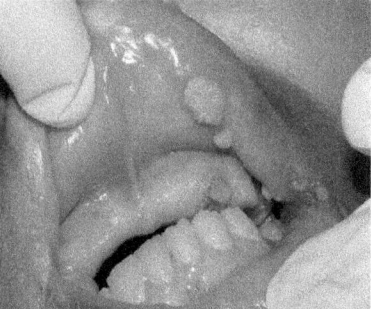

Gonorrhea

Gonorrhea: Consists of persistent pus discharge from vagina, inflammation of entire genital passage, burning and discomfort are symptoms of Gonorrhea - a fatal venereal disease usually transmitted by sexual contact caused by a tiny bean-shaped germ called a 'gonococcus' in both men and women.

Causes: The disease may also be contracted from contaminated hands, instruments, clothing, toilet seats, and even bath water. The disese is transmitted during sexual intercourse. If mother in infected with this disease, there is danger of newborn infant contracting this disease.

Symptoms: Burning on urination, urge to frequent urination, a profuse greenish-yellow discharge, red and swollen end of the penis in males in males and hot, swollen opening to the vagina along with thick yellow discharge in women are some of the symptoms of this disease.

Treatment: Penicillin or Terramycin is the best drugs recommended for the treatment of this fatal disease (strictly under the guidance of a doctor as there may be a reaction due to these drugs). A Hip Bath in hot water is useful. Urethra should be flushed with a solution of potassium permanganate (1:3000) with the help of a syringe to be kept in urethra for five minutes. The patient should avoid constipation. Sex should be strictly forbidden.

Genital Herpes: Herpes simplex virus produces infection generally passed on through sexual contact. Appearance of blisters on genital areas, thighs, buttocks, fever, body ache, weakness, thick vaginal discharge, irritation, urinary burning and enlarged lymph nodes are some of the symptoms of this disease. Different sized vesicles and reddish ulcers appear in the vulvae region. Women who practice rectal sex also develop the lesions in the area around the anus and higher up in the rectum.

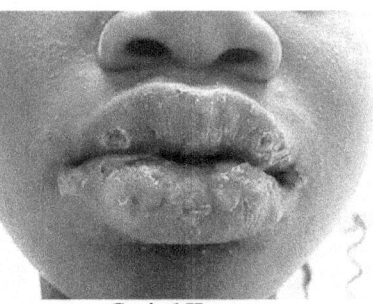
Genital Herpes

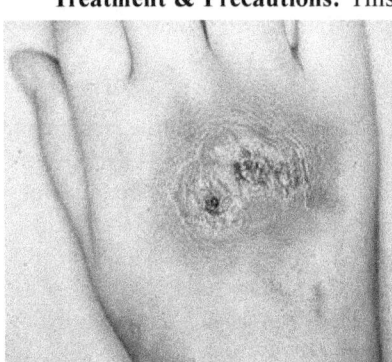
Fungus Infection

Treatment & Precautions: This disease is treated by the application of anti-viral cream or a lotion. Use condoms during sexual intercourse. Take bath in warm water. Worry, depression and lack of sleep are biggest enemies during the attack of this disease. Soothe the affected skin with essential oil (diluted in a base oil) of lemon, geranium, chamomile or lavender. The oil should be gently rubbed on to the rash.

Fungus infection: Occasionally, the female genital organs of a pregnant woman get infected with fungus because of the increased sugar content in the blood. Women suffering from diabetes are more likely to have fungus infections resulting in intense itching around the genital area and a thick discharge from the vagina. Take a warm vinegar douche once or twice a day in consultation with your doctor.

Candida: Females during reproductive age sometimes suffer from candida. Factors like the state of pregnancy, diabetes, administration of antibiotics

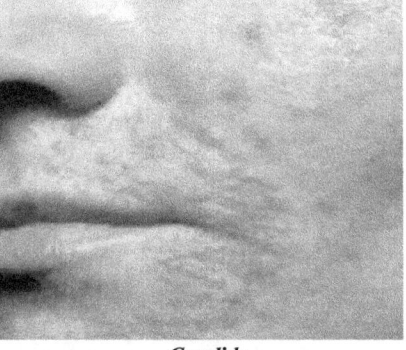
Candida

and steroids and use of contraceptive pills cause this disorder, which produces white vaginal discharge with intense irritation and burning sensation.

Treatment: To treat affected area, apply anti-fungal cream recommended for both men and women to eliminate the fungus and prevent re-infection from the sex partner. In case of females, doctors generally recommend tablets inserted intra-vaginally.

Thrush (Vulva Viginitis): Thrush is infection usually develops in the gastro-intestinal tract. Whitish curd-like deposits appear on the tongue. The thrush infection of vagina is known as vulva vaginitis, which cause itching, redness and discharge. The vaginal infection can be transmitted to the male partner and vice versa.

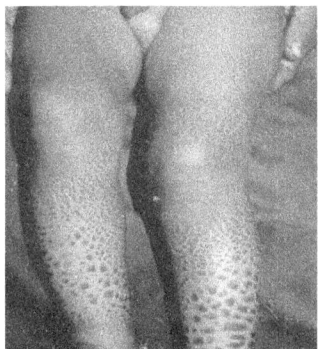
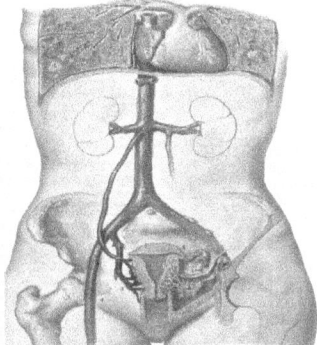
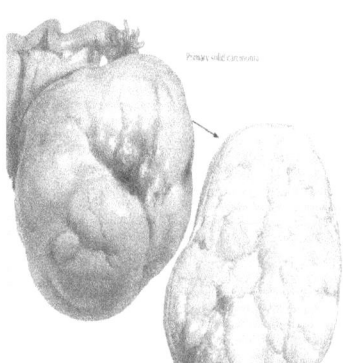

Thrush (Vulva Viginitis)

Symptoms of vaginitis include:

- ▶ Pain, redness and itching into the vagina and vulva.
- ▶ Severe pain when urinating and involved in sexual intercourse.
- ▶ Foul smelling white or blood-streaked discharge.
- ▶ Pelvic inflammation resulting in infertility.

The following measures are taken for the treatment of vaginitis (strictly as prescribed by your doctor):

- ▶ Avoid wearing nylon panties, tight jeans and a moist environment around genital area.
- ▶ Avoid sugar, refined carbohydrates and alcohol, which turn into glucose in the body.
- ▶ Eat 100 gm of unsweetened yogurt daily.
- ▶ Garlic is antibacterial, anti-fungal that fights both bacterial vaginitis and candidiasis. Take one capsule once or twice a day.
- ▶ Insert a 600 mg capsule of boric acid powder into vagina twice a day for a week. To prevent recurrence insert one capsule daily at bed time for four days during menstrual period. Do not insert capsule in case of pregnancy.
- ▶ Insert a vitamin E capsule into the vagina once or twice a day for seven days, which is soothing to vaginal tissue, decreases irritation, redness, swelling and congestion.
- ▶ Ayurvedic herb 'triphla' helps remove toxins from the body and helps in treating a yeast infection. Soak ½ teaspoon of dried herb in 1 cup of hot water for five minutes. Drink the liquid at night before sleep. Douching, too, dries the vagina.

Some Querries

How to cure small papules accompanied with intense itching on the organ of my husband?

These are probably lesions of scabies seen on genitals organ with intense itching. These lesions are observed as papules on the prepuce, glans, shaft of penis and scrotum in male organs. Female genitalia are rarely involved. Surface warts also do occur on genitalia.

I suffer from genital warts. Suggest treatment for the same

Genital warts are usually transmitted by sexual contact or through infection from the hands and nail, as such both the partners should keep hands clean when having sex. Warts can occur in both sexes and are usually located on the moist surface of genitalia. Initially, they appear as minute reddish swellings growing in groups of lesions. The genital warts should be treated with the consultation of a good doctor.

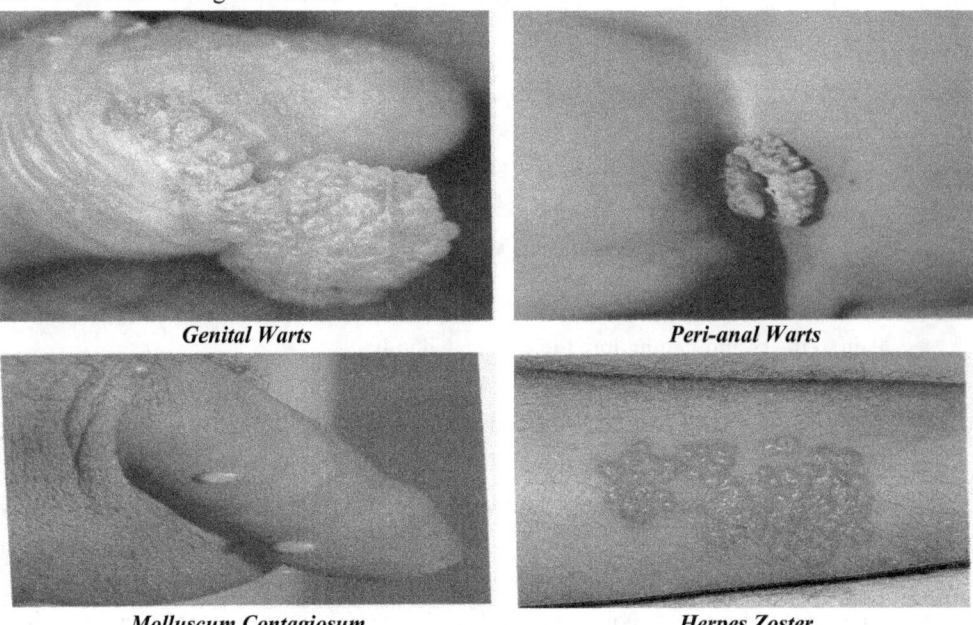

Genital Warts   *Peri-anal Warts*

Molluscum Contagiosum   *Herpes Zoster*

Remedies to genital herpes are caused by a virus, in which groups of little blisters appear on the genital area, thighs and buttocks. The following natural remedies for genital herpes are recommended:

Vitamins and minerals: A herpes outbreak is a sign that your body is under stress and needs more nutrients. The following nutrient program may help reduce the stress, shorten the herpes attack and reduce its severity:

- ▶ Vitamin A: Daily dose of 20,000 IU twice for a week.
- ▶ Vitamin B Complex: Daily dose 50 mg for a month.
- ▶ Vitamin C: Daily dose 500 to 1000 mg three times a day for 2 weeks.
- ▶ Vitamin E: 400 IU twice a day for two weeks.

- Zinc: 10 mg twice a day for a week.
- Calcium/Magnesium: 500 mg of calcium and 250 mg of magnesium twice a day for a month.
- Selenium: 200 micrograms daily for two weeks.
- Drink water as much as you can, which helps flush toxins out of the body that weaken immune system and allow the virus to reactivate.
- Soothe group of little blisters appearing on genital area with essential oils (diluted in a base oil) of lemon, geranium, chamomile or lavender.
- Common warts are treated by electro-cautery, which excises the warts with electric current.

Remember, warts should be diagnosed accurately and treated early rather than waiting until they spread and enlarge and are more difficult to eliminate. Genital warts can be sexually transmitted and may be a risk factor for cervical cancer in women. The following natural remedies are suggested:

- Garlic oil is a traditional remedy for warts. Swab the oil on the wart or on a bandage applied to the wart.
- Remove warts with cryosurgery or freezing with liquid nitrogen or carbon snow.

How to cure severe itching in/around the genital area during night hours?

You suffer from scabies: a contagious disease caused by a mite, which lays eggs in burrows in the skin. The disease spreads through contact with infected individual. The commonly affected parts of the body are finger webs, wrist, arms, buttocks, lower abdomen, thighs, breast-folds, female genital area and penis (in men). There is severe itching on the affected area at night and sometimes thin, slimy fluid oozes out of the scratched surface and scabs. To treat scabby following remedies are advised:

- Boil leaves of oleander (Karbir) till charred in 250 ml mustard oil and massage the affected skin.
- Mix juices of lemon and jasmine in equal quantity and rub on the itching skin.
- Grind poppy seeds in water. Mix to it lime juice. Massage affected skin with the paste.

I suffer from abscess or a yellow cyst on labia majora or the vaginal area having swelling. Suggest a remedy.

Probably, you suffer from Bartholin's gland - a vulva disease, causing abscesses or cysts due to infection during reproductive years including pregnancy with the signs and symptoms like painful swelling of labia, formation of abscess or on vagina with clear or yellow or blue cysts at the base of the labia majora. To prevent the disease avoid or reduce exposure to sexually transmitted diseases and vulva trauma. Better consult your doctor to avoid expansion of the disease and increase in swelling.

I often have severe irritation on the genital area. Can you suggest a remedy?

You may be suffering from Contact Vulvitis in which there is often vulva irritation during pregnancy period caused by the factors like severe irritation, un-hygienic conditions common during pregnancy, ill-effect of deodorants and soaps used on genital area, wearing tight-fitting and synthetic under-garments, tampons or pads, using perfumes, scented toilet paper, laundry soap, effect of condoms, lubricants, topical contraceptives and sexual aids used during pregnancy. Sometimes, trouble causes due to frequent vaginal secretions during pregnancy or semen remains in the vagina for a long time after having sex and soiling of vulva by urine or faces.

The signs and symptoms of this disorder include severe dermatitis of vulva, reddening of vulva skin accompanied by itching and burning, vulva dystrophy and excessive vaginal secretions.

Dysareunia insertional is another common disorder in women during the pregnancy in reproductive age. It is caused due to several factors such as inadequate lubrication in vaginal canal, phobias while having sex, pelvis muscle spasm, scarring in the vaginal canal, surgical repairs to the vulva and effect of herpes vulvitis. The disorder leads to severe burning or pinching. Treatment includes vaginal lubrication, regular practice of pelvic techniques to reduce pain during sexual intercourse.

What to do in case of recurrent inflammation on labia with severe pain?

These are signs of Hidradenitis Suppurative disease due to a chronic refractory infection of the skin and subcutaneous tissues causing inflammation and formation of abscess on vulva and perineum with recurrent inflammation, severe pain, foul smelling discharge and sometimes formation of abscess.

General measures for the treatment of this disease are perineal hygiene, a Sitz's bath, administering antibiotics in consultation with a doctor, avoidingformation of the scar or a abscesses. Remember, it is a infectious disorder.

Feel thickening on vulva skin over the labia majora, labia minora and clitorial area?

If the symptoms include inflammation, irritation, itching, fissuring and excoriations, the disorder may be Vulva Dystrophy. If not timely treated can cause cancer of the vulva and chronic vulvitis. To treat this disorder one requires measures like perineal hygiene, reducing stress and reduction of contact allergy. On should strictly follow precautions such as wearing gloves during night to avoid tissue damages due to scratching. Avoid itching and scratching.

The disorder may further lead to Lichen Sclerosus - a chronic condition causing vulva inflammation generally during pregnancy, late reproductive age and during early menopausal when there is intense itching, scratch marks or fissures around the anus. Perineal hygiene, a Sitz's bath and application of petroleum jelly and some of the measures to treat this disorder If not treated timely, complications such as cancer of vulva, scarring and narrowing of the vaginal canal resulting in surgical delivery may arise.

Doctor says I am suffering from Vulva Hematoma, what's that and how to treat it?

The disease consists of swelling of one or both labia because of interstitial bleeding due to sexual intercourse or after a rape during pregnancy. Sometimes, it is due to varicose veins of vulva or hard labour activities. The signs and symptoms of this disease are painful swelling of one or both labia, dark blue or black discoloration of vulva, bleeding and formation of cysts and abscess. To treat the disorder, apply ice packs on vulva. Surgical drainage is necessary in case of rapidly expanding symptoms.

Vaginal Diseases

Why vaginal diseases like Cystocele, Urethrocele and Rectocele occur and how to treat these conditions?

Cysocdele and Urethrocele are vaginal diseases caused by lack of support due to ruptured vagina, pro-lapse of the urethra or bladder due to loss of normal tissue integrity caused by previous surgical childbirth or a obstetric injury, pressure on the pelvic region, urinary

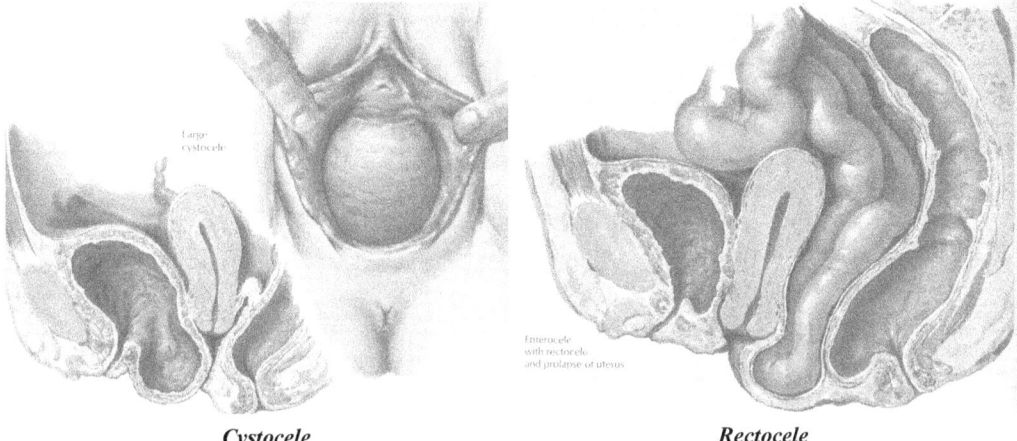

              Cystocele   *Rectocele*

infections, formation of cysts, tumours and abscess on urethra. Measures like weight-reduction, pelvic muscle exercises. surgical repairs, avoiding heavy lifting and straining are important measures to treat this disorder. Consult a doctor immediately in case vaginal bleeding and symptoms of breast cancer.

    Rectocele is caused due to failure of the normal support mechanism between the rectum and the vagina due to childbirth, obesity, heavy lifting and weakness of intrinsic tissue. The main signs and symptoms of this disease are bulging of posterior vaginal wall, difficulty in passing stool, risk of a rectal cancer, vaginal cyst and uterine pro-lapse. Weight loss, systemic estrogen replacement, pelvic muscle exercises and surgical repair are some of the measures to treat this disorder.

Have cysts on vaginal area. What to do?

It is a common disorder in females from adolescence to middle reproductive years generally caused due to factors e.g. episiotomy (vaginal cut during previous delivery) or in gynecologic surgery. Cystic lesions ranging up to 5 cm. are found in the lateral vaginal wall. Surgical excision is the only reliable treatment. Better consult your doctor.

Feel irritation, itching and pain due to vaginal dryness. Can you suggest a remedy?

Loss of normal vaginal moisture cause irritation, itching and pain during sexual intercourse and inflamed vaginal tissue are prominent signs and symptoms of this disorder. Vaginal dryness occurs due to inadequate or inappropriate sexual stimulation, sexual phobia or pain more common in pregnant or menopausal women. Some prominent measures to treat such dryness are topical moisturizing, lubrication of vagina, estrogen replacement therapy and use of water-soluble lubricants before intercourse. If not treated properly, it may lead to vaginal lacerations, infections, vulva excoriations and sexual dysfunction.

What is the reason of vaginal bleeding and persistent pain after the intercourse?

Vaginal Laceriation is caused due to frequent sexual intercourse during pregnancy usually under the influence of alcohol and drugs causing injury and penetration by foreign objects, which cause vaginal bleeding, persistent pain after the intercourse, cervical polyp, bleeding and sometimes threatened abortion. To treat it, have pelvic rest and avoid sex until healing occurs.

I find Vaginal Pro-lapse and have to seek the help of a doctor. Suggest how to avoid.

Vaginal pro-lapse occurs due to loss of normal support to foetus resulting in vaginal wall-down in vaginal canal when in extreme cases vagina is displaced beyond the vulva outside the body. Frequent childbirth, intra-abdominal pressure, heavy lifting and intrinsic tissue weakness is the prominent causes of vaginal pro-lapse. Regular pelvic pain, uterus dyspareunia, bleeding and vaginal cyst or tumour is sign and symptoms of this disorder.

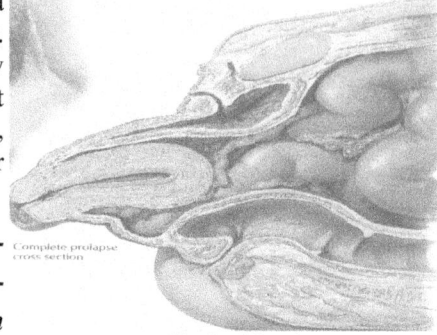

Vaginal Pro-lapse

I am four months pregnant. Itching, irritation and inflammation are common symptoms. My doctor says I'm suffering from Bacterial Vaginitis. How to get rid of this problem?

A vaginal infection caused by excessive growth of bacteria generally causes severe itching, irritation and inflammation in genital area in females between the age of 15 to 50, most common during pregnancy due to suffering from diabetes, pregnancy and debilitating disease, habit of too much smoking in some women, frequent intercourse during pregnancy period, effect of excess number of sexual partners, too much use of vaginal contraceptives, oral sex, and unhygienic conditions especially during pregnancy. Perineal hygiene is an important measure to treat this disorder. If neglected, the possible complications like cystitis (desire of frequent urination), cervicitis, severe infections, pelvic inflammatory disease, pelvic pain, infertility, increased risk of upper genital-tract infection, premature delivery and premature rupture of the membranes may take place. A pregnant woman should immediately seek the consultation of a gynecologist.

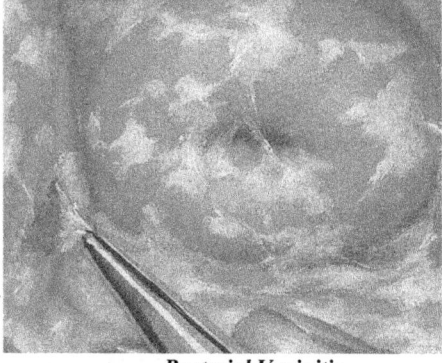

Bacterial Vaginitis

Why is the problem of Vaginitis-Monilial common in females?

A vaginal infection caused by fungi found in the atmosphere at vagina, rectum and vaginal mouth usually occurs in females between the age 15 to 50 years generally during the period of pregnancy due to frequent secretions. Nearly 80 to 90 % cases of this vaginal disease are caused due to candida albicus, candida glabrata or candida tropicals. Those suffering from this disorder should avoid stress, diabetes, depression, topical contraceptives and warm and moist environment.

Thrush (Vulva Viginitis)

The patients face symptoms such as vulva itching or burning, scratching, edema, vulva excoriations, white to yellow thick pussy discharge and pinworms. Perineal hygiene, keeping the affected area clean and dry are the main precautions to treat this disorder. Avoid wearing tight synthetic undergarments and use of topical steroid preparations if you suffer from this disorder.

Itching, burning and yellow to green colour foul odour discharge on the vulva are some of the symptoms. Suggest suitable remedy to treat it.

Your are probably suffering from Vaginitis Trichomonas - a vaginal infection in pregnant women generally caused by having too much sex, less acid in blood and semen (vaginal pH). If

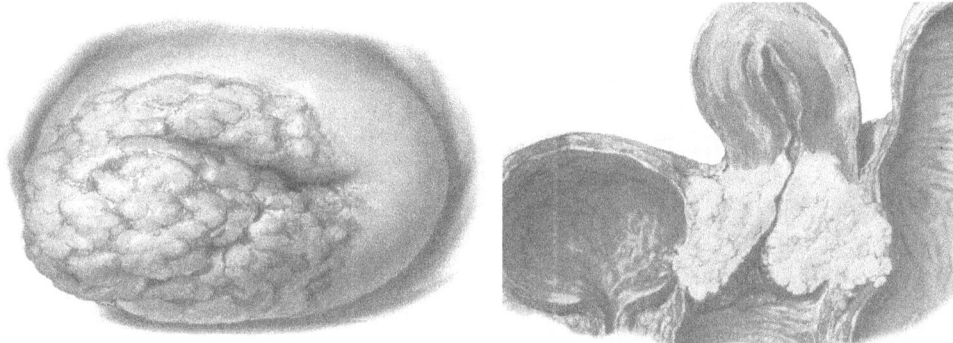

Vaginitis Trichomonas

not treated properly, it leads to complications like cystitis (inflammation of the bladder resulting in frequent urge to pass urine), pain in lower abdomen, pelvic inflammation and pelvic pain. This disorder can be cured by medical treatment only. Consult a doctor immediately.

What to do in case of carcinoma in cervix and cervix cancer?

Carcinoma in cervix in reproductive age or during pregnancy is harmful and may lead to vaginitis, cervicitis and cervical dysplasia. Consult your doctor for the treatment who usually suggest a Pap smears examination, cryo-therapy, electro-cautery and electro-surgical loop excision for treatments, but these are very harmful during pregnancy.

The prominent causes of this disorder are herpes virus, early sexual activities, too much or multiple sexual partners, use of oral contraceptives and early childbearing. Measures to treat the disease are standard hysterectomy, ablative therapy, cryosurgery and CO_2 laser therapy. Seek advice of a doctor as these treatments are very harmful for pregnant women.

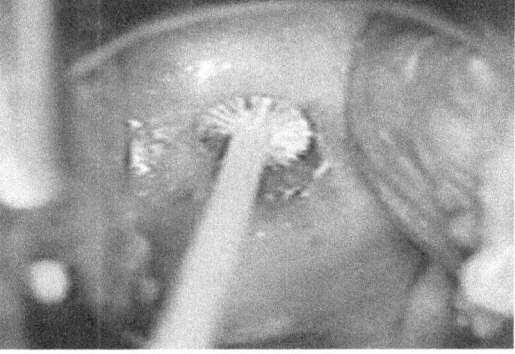

Cervix Cancer

Remember, almost all cancers of cervix are carcinoma. The disease is often seen in women during pregnancy and is generally caused due to early sexual activities, too much or multiple sex partners and presence of sexually transmitted viral infections. Signs and symptoms of the disease include abnormal Pap smear, vaginal bleeding, dark vaginal discharge, loss of appetite, weight loss, bleeding lesion, inguinal lymph nodes, swelling of legs, cervical erosion and cervical polyp. Chemotherapy is curative measure to treat the disease, but seek advice of a doctor for treatment.

Does pregnancy cause cancer in women?

No in women two most likely places where cancer may develop includes the *breasts and the uterus*. Both areas can easily be examined. Every young woman should be taught to examine her own breasts after each menstrual period. In case of detection of a tumour or anything unusual, a woman should seek advice of doctor. Any kind of abnormality or feeling of the breast tissue outlining the curves within the breasts and up in the armpit should be examined thoroughly. Cancer of the cervix, breast or uterus is most common in women. Over 40% females suffer from cervical cancer, nearly 12% from breast cancer and the remaining cancer patients are seen suffering from vaginal or cancer of the other parts of body.

Breast Tumour and Cancer: is very common in women of every age. If there is only one single nodule or lump in the breasts: painful or without pain, it should always be removed. In case the cancer appears to have extended into the neighboring lymph nodes, the patient should be given extensive radiation therapy. Majority of breast cancers occur in either the upper portion of the breast, towards the shoulder or close to the nipple. Breast cancer is more common in women between the age of 35 and 65 years. It may also occur in teenage girls.

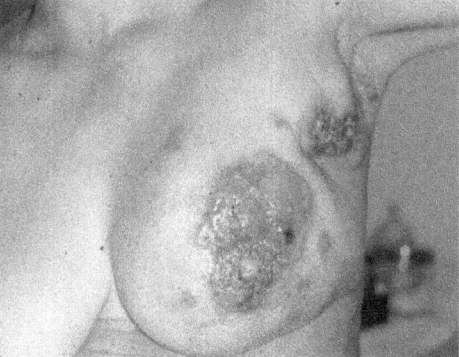

Breast Tumour and Cancer

Cancer in Cervix is a vicious killer of woman today. Every female after the age 18 should have a pelvic examination and a Pap smear at least once a year or after six months. Any pain in the lower belly or a water discharge should be investigated, as it could be a cancer. Be careful, if the bleeding or spotting follows intercourse or douching. Modern treatment for the uterine cancer consists of implanting a small amount of radium within the cervical canal followed later by heavy dose of radiation therapy to the whole area. Performing a hysterectomy, removing the uterus, cervix, ovaries and tubes are the common treatments performed when suffering from a cervical cancer.

Cancer in Uterus: is less common type of cancer, known as fundal carcinoma. It may sometimes develop within the cavity of uterus itself. This is less malignant than cancer of the cervix and can be detected by Pap smear. If cancer is found, a hysterectomy should be done without delay. The cancer cells find their way into the abdominal cavities and may spread to the pelvis and eventually in the whole body.

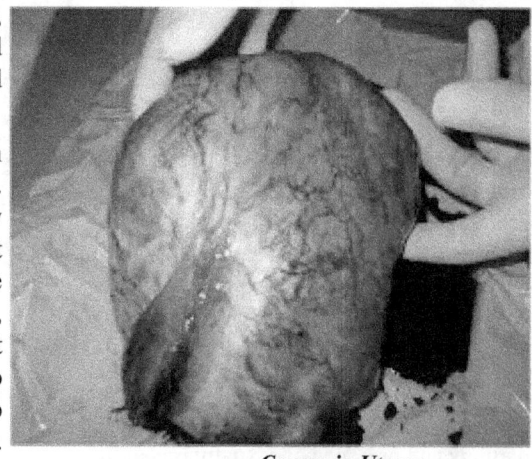

Cancer in Uterus

Vaginal Diseases

Ovarian Cysts and Cancer: is most frequent tumour in the body. Every woman has a small cyst on the ovary, which may disappear spontaneously. The ovarian cyst causes distension

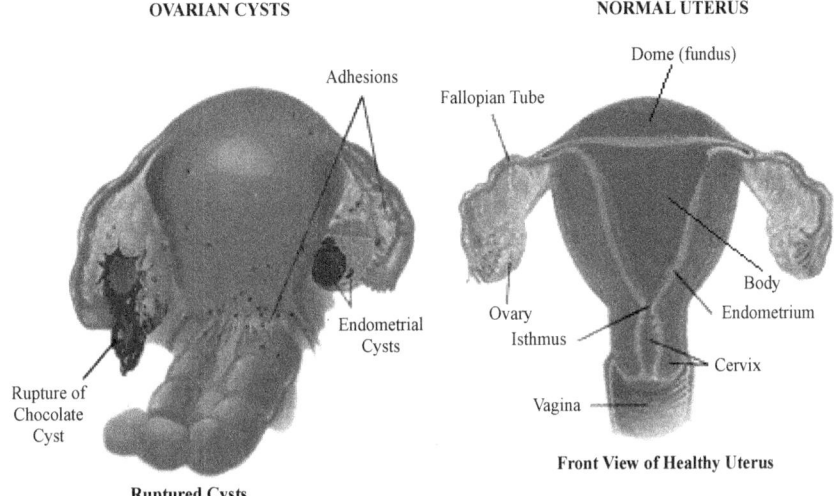

Ovarian Cysts

of the abdomen and pressure on the organs such as the bladder or rectum. It should be removed by surgery without delay. *Cancer may develop in the wall of ovarian cyst,* and may spread to other nearby organs causing obstruction of the bowels.

Chapter-10

Important Tips for the New Born

What should be the weight of the newly born baby?

First weight of a live or stillborn baby taken within the first hour of life before any postnatal weight loss occurs. Babies with a birth weight of less than 2500 g irrespective of the period of gestation are known as low birth weight (LBW) babies. Babies with less than 2000 g weight are considered as high risk and are admitted to the special care neonatal unit (SCNU). Babies with a birth weight of less than 1500 g are known as very low birth weight (VLBW) babies. The babies with a birth weight of less than 1000 g are known as extremely low birth weight (ELBW) babies.

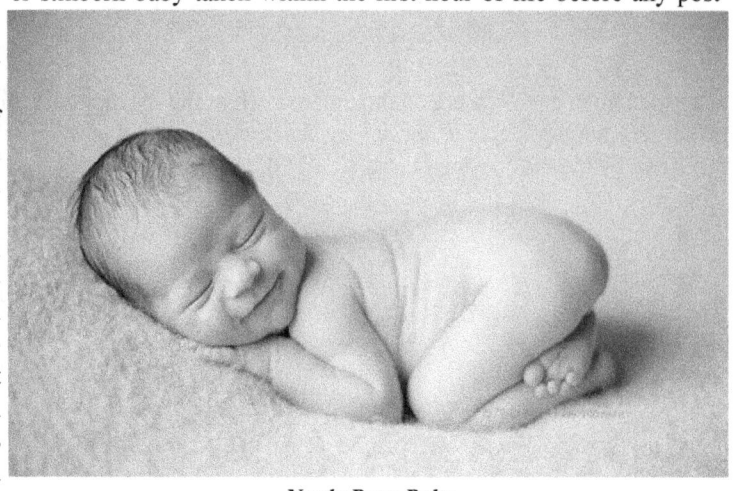

Newly Born Baby

What is an incubator?

This is essential to provide an ideal micro-environment of high-risk babies. The main functions of a incubator isolation are maintenance of thermo-neutral ambient temperature, desired humidity and administration of oxygen. The following newborn babies are transferred to special care nursery without delay:

▶ Birth weight of a baby is less than 2000 g

- Gestation of less than 36 weeks
- Birth asphyxia.
- Rhesus iso-immunization.
- Gross congenital malformations.
- Respiratory distress.
- Maternal diabetes. Mellitus.
- Unwell or unwilling mother.

What are the necessary examinations of a baby at birth?

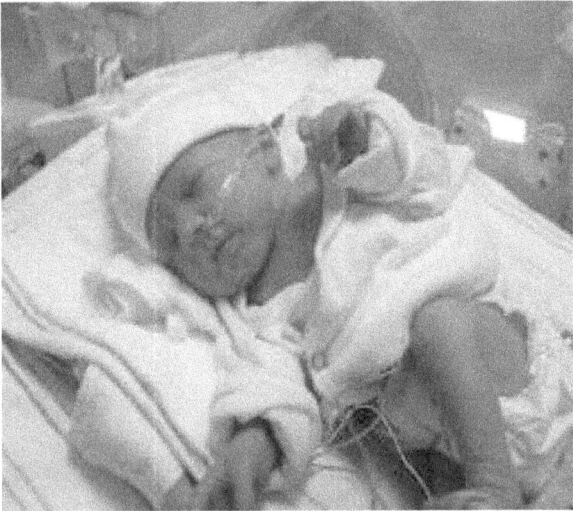

Baby in an Incubator

Conduct examinations of the baby undressed in a warm, comfortable room placed on a flat surface having good sources of light within 24 hours of birth to check birth weight, general behavior such as color, respirations, movement of limbs and their posture. Also check skull (head circumference is more than 3 cm. bigger than chest), any facial deformity, skin of the body, spine and other body organs. Do not forget to check feet or any deformities in abdomen, genitalia, heart, chest, hips to find out congenital dislocation.

Closely watched the following deformities:

- Bleeding from any site
- Appearance of jaundice within 24 hours after birth
- Failure to pass meconium by infant within 24 hours
- Failure to pass urine within 48 hours
- Vomiting or diarrhea
- Excessive crying by baby
- Poor feeding
- Excessive frothiness or drooling
- Choking at feeds
- Respiratory difficulty and/or cyanosis
- Sudden rise or fall in the body temperature
- Any evidence of superficial infection

The schedule of immunization is as following:

Age	Vaccine
0-7 days	BCG, OPV
6th week	OPV, DPT
10th week	OPV, DPT
14th week	OPV, DTP

9th month	Measles
15th month	MMR
18th month	OPV, DPT
24th month	TAB (2 doses at an interval of 2 weeks)
School entry	OPV, DPT, BCG
Mid school	TAB and Tetanus toxoid (every 3-5 years)

What are the common neo-natal problems?

You must consult your doctor immediately in case of the following problems:

- ▶ Vomiting.
- ▶ Failure to pass urine.
- ▶ Bowel disorders e.g. constipation and diarrhea.
- ▶ Physiological jaundice.
- ▶ Dehydration fever.
- ▶ Superficial infections.
- ▶ Excessive crying.
- ▶ Excessive sleepiness.
- ▶ Disorders due to trans-placental passage of hormones e.g. mastitis neonatrum on 3rd or 4th day, vaginal menstruation like bleeding after 3 to 5 days lasting 2 to 4 days of birth and mucoid vaginal secretions.
- ▶ Cephalhematoma (subperiasteal collection of blood due to injury during delivery).
- ▶ Umbilical granuloma (small red flesh like nodule at the base of umbilicus with persistent discharge).
- ▶ Wetness or watering from eyes.
- ▶ Sore buttocks and napkin rashes usually due to use of nylon or tight plastic nappies.
- ▶ Various minor developmental peculiarities e.g. rashes, dry peeling skin, spots patch (stork-bites), subconjunctival hemorrhage, sucking callosities, tongue-tie, umbilical hernia and bowed legs.

There may be few physiological handicaps, which should also be brought in the notice of your doctor:

- ▶ Central nervous system
- ▶ Respiratory system
- ▶ Cardiovascular system
- ▶ Gastrointestinal system
- ▶ Thermo-regulation (hypothermia)
- ▶ Infections
- ▶ Renal immaturity
- ▶ Nutritional handicaps causing anaemia

▶ Biochemical disturbances

What are advantages of breastfeeding and what are the common types of breast milk?
These include the following:
- ▶ Free from contamination and adulteration
- ▶ Easily digestible
- ▶ Convenient during night
- ▶ Possesses anti-infective properties (low incidence and infective, diarrhea, respiratory infection, milk allergy and risk of eczema)
- ▶ Less likely to develop obesity and hypertension
- ▶ Helps in spacing the birth of babies
- ▶ Protects breast cancer
- ▶ Promotes better figure
- ▶ Free of cost feeding

The types of breast milk are as following:
- ▶ *Colostrum*: Yellow thick milk secreted during the first three days after delivery, which contains more antibodies, white blood cells and contains higher protein.

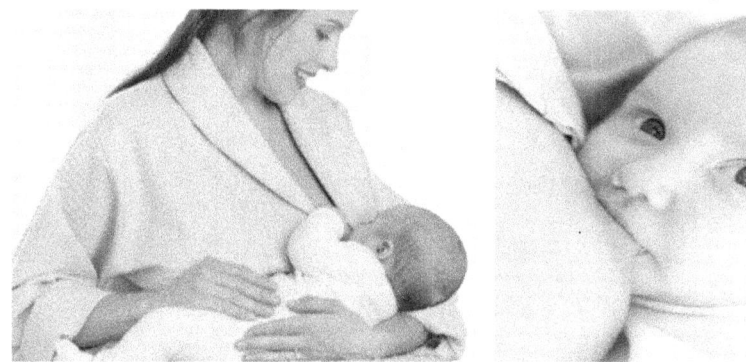

Types of Breast Milk

- ▶ *Transitional milk:* Milk secreted during the following two weeks after colostrums.
- ▶ *Mature milk:* Milk follows transitional milk, which contains all thin watery nutrients essential for optimal growth of body.
- ▶ *Pre-term milk:* The mothers milk who had delivered baby prematurely, contains more calories, higher concentration of fat, protein and sodium needed by pre-term baby.
- ▶ *Fore milk:* Watery and rich in proteins, sugar, vitamins and minerals milk secreted at the start of a feed, which is richer in fat content and provide more energy.

What are some of the recommendations for a successful breastfeeding of a child?
- ▶ Retracted and cracked nipples must be managed before delivery.
- ▶ The first feed should be breast mi8lk. No water, honey, glucose, water, tea etc.

- ▶ Breastfeeding should be started in the first hour of life.
- ▶ Hold baby in the correct position.
- ▶ Feed the baby in comfortable position.
- ▶ Rooming-in is a must for successful lactation.
- ▶ Feed baby on demand not by clock.
- ▶ Avoid bottle feed as far as possible.
- ▶ Breastfed baby does not require supplementation with water.
- ▶ Frequent suckling, emptying of breast completely, correct position, while feeding and supportive care are some of the causes of *successful lactation*.

www.ingramcontent.com/pod-product-compliance
Lightning Source LLC
Chambersburg PA
CBHW080553230426
43663CB00015B/2818